Confidence Changed My Life

Table of Contents

INTRODUCTION

Confidence can represent the difference between a life lived well and life merely lived. Individuals who have self-esteem have better social skills, are better able to control their emotions, and are more resilient. Although confidence may seem like an easy thing to obtain, for many people it is actually quite elusive. A famous psychoanalyst believed that most human beings have an inferiority complex, and for the person dealing with anxiety, this inferiority complex can seem like an insurmountable obstacle. As society has changed, more and more men and women seem to be dealing with issues of confidence rendering the subject of how to build it more critical.

Indeed, the world seems to be changing at a breakneck pace and it can be a struggle merely to keep up. The days where people around the world sent letters to one another have long gone. Now, men and women worldwide communicate instantly via email, mobile phones, and instant messaging. And technological advancement has not stopped there. A future where artificial intelligence is a part of our daily lives has become increasingly imminent. Daily on television, we see images of an increasingly changing, and increasingly chaotic, world. Even the most resilient person may find it more and more difficult to find joy and satisfaction in the same ways that they did in the past.

Indeed, a phenomenon taking place in Japan seems to shed light on the changing technological world and how it may be impacting otherwise ordinary folk. This is the phenomenon of the hermit, the man or woman who lives in their tiny apartment in big cities like Tokyo and Osaka and never leaves the house. These hermits, or hikikomori, are frequently men, but sometimes women, who rarely if ever leave their apartments. Often described as "sexless," this hikikomori represents not only how Japan has changed, but how the world at large has begun to morph into something different.

It is believed that half a million people in Japan live as hikikomori. Hikikomori is a term from the Japanese language, which means to hide in yourself or to retreat. These are people that are not only isolated spatially but socially. There is also psychological isolation, a very important concept in this book as we explore the ways that men and women can build confidence and become more resilient. Isolation can be hard to overcome, but it is important as the state of being isolated can worsen low self-esteem and any underlying mental condition that a person is dealing with.

Hikikomori lives detached from the world, which is why we think of them as hermits. Some of these hermits live with family members but never leave their bedrooms. Others live completely alone, making them entirely isolated and disconnected from the outside world. This phenomenon primarily impacts younger Japanese, those people who, it would seem, should be better able to handle the rapidly changing world because they were born into it.

But the fact that most of these hermits are young people seems to be revelatory about why this phenomenon has come to exist in the first place. Japanese society has always been competitive and it has only grown to be more so. Japanese people compete to get into the best universities and then they compete for spots at the best companies where, in many cases, they are expected to spend the rest of their adult lives until retirement.

But rather than embark on this roller coaster ride that is normalcy in Japan, the hikikomori has withdrawn from the world, spending their time playing video games and watching television. The problem has become so severe that rehabilitation centers designed to treat such people have appeared. And lest one think that this problem is confined to Japan, centers to treat "video game addiction" have also appeared in the United States, though men and women stateside perhaps have not made the link between video game playing and underlying social issues of increased societal competitiveness and lack of confidence.

Not all of the hikikomori are young people. Indeed, the phenomenon of hermit life has spread outside the under 30 demographics in Japan. And lest one think that these hermits are like the hermits of the Middle Ages who never left their monastery cells, the hikikomori often says that they feel physically ill if they are unable to hear the sound of the television or of a video game. The silence can remind the hermits that they are alone, the isolation that troubles them.

Indeed, though the term hikikomori implies that the individual living in this state seeks isolation, in fact, many have become isolated as they are unable to deal with the world for various reasons. Many of these individuals have problems of depression or anxiety that have been exacerbated by the increasingly competitive, technologically advanced, and highly visual society that characterizes the modern world. The depression and anxiety of the hikikomori combined with a lack of confidence and resilience keep them trapped in their uncomfortable world.

For the person dealing with depression, anxiety, or any issue that impacts their sense of self-worth, building confidence is not a luxury but a necessity. The point here is that thinking about self-esteem and taking steps to build it up has become increasingly more important in the modern world. Although social scientists are not entirely sure why technological advancement seems to be making people more isolated rather than less so, this phenomenon has been noted and the hikikomori of Japan stands out as a sterling example of what happens when steps are not taken.

In Confidence Changed My Life, the critical importance of investing in self-esteem and confidence will be explored. Although building self-esteem seems to be merely a question of taking steps to improve one's sense of self-worth, for many people confidence-building actually begins with identifying those things that are impacting your confidence and overcoming. Indeed, many people who lack confidence have social anxiety, a sense of inferiority, or feel isolated from others so recognizing this and acting on it is an important first step.

Why is it important to build confidence at all? Well, leaving aside the fate of the hikikomori who feel great isolation and disconnection (and are perceptive of this), confidence is important in achieving personal success in life and being happy. Whether they admit it or not, the goal of most people is to be happy. Although achieving happiness may not entail the same steps for everyone, reaching the point where you feel good about where you are and who you are representing the ultimate goal for a human being, what social scientists refer to as self-actualization. Confidence, therefore, is an important piece of feeling fulfilled as a human being and being happy.

An important player in confidence is mindfulness. Mindfulness can be thought of as a type of awareness that allows people to recognize how they are feeling and to act on this feeling if need be. Although some people are naturally confident and may not need to check in on themselves to halt negative feelings and boost their confidence, for many people this is an important step. Sure, the naturally confident people of the world seem to have it easy, but it is important to remember that many of the most successful people of the world were not born with the advantages that naturally give people confidence. Most of these successful people had to overcome challenges, which means they had to draw from a deep well of self-esteem and, in some cases, find ways to motivate themselves and build confidence.

For many of the most successful people, having self-esteem and making their own way in the world meant overcoming the negative thinking that can keep people from reaching their full potential. Our own thoughts can be our worst enemy, keeping us in a negative mindset that prevents us from taking the necessary steps and making critical changes in our lives. It becomes important, therefore, to be conscious of our thoughts and when our thoughts are problematic. These thoughts can be as simple as "I am not good at this" or "I always do this." One of the worst offenders is "I will never be able to do this" or "this is impossible." As commonplace and typical as these phrases may be in everyday parlance, these words and phrases have a power: in this case, the power to keep us from achieving our goals.

Negative thinking goes even further than that. This type of thinking does not have to feature the sort of absolutes that were mentioned in the examples above. For many people, negative thinking can take the form of assuming that things will turn out badly because they turned out badly before or thinking about the bad sides of a situation instead of the good ones. For example, a person who loses their job may say: “This always happens. I will never be able to keep a good job.” This is negative thinking that actually can create a cycle of failed endeavors and unhappiness. A more confident, resilient person would say: “This job did not work out the way I thought it would but I know it is for the best. There are more opportunities out there and my perfect job is within reach.” The difference here is that the first person is seeing the situation he or she is in as a hopelessly negative one while the second person realizes that a job that did not work out is really just an opportunity to get an even better one.

So, what is the relationship between this type of thinking, confidence, and success? Negative thinking in the form of cognitive distortions leads people to perceive themselves, their lives, and the world in a way that is negative instead of seeing the positive opportunities. We all trip and fall in our lives, but success can be a matter of how well the individual is able to pick themselves back up again and keep moving. A person with a negative mindset will fall and may never be able to pick themselves back up. This negative mindset is tied to a lack of confidence because such a person does not perceive that they are not their circumstances. Things may be bad now but that does not mean they always have to be so.

There is also an element of unreality in this type of thinking. The person who thinks negatively does not actually see things as they are. For example, a person who personalizes the situation may interpret a coworker who does not greet them as a sign that no one at the office likes them and they are likely to lose their job soon. They will ruminate about how unfair this situation is and may even quit their job to prevent being fired first. This is unrealistic because a bad interaction with someone does not necessarily mean all of the things that someone personalizing the situation thinks it means. Just as we have bad days and are not always able to be friendly to others so too do others find themselves in the same situation.

In the previous example, the person who thought that their job was in jeopardy because a coworker did not greet them as they would have liked was engaging in at least two cognitive distortions: personalizing and catastrophizing (not to mention others). They personalized a situation that probably had nothing to do with them and then they blew everything out of proportion. It is not difficult to see why thinking and behaving this way is problematic. It not only causes us to misinterpret the simplest of events, but it can leave us feeling hopelessly socially isolated, not unlike the hikikomori of Japan.

It may be difficult to see the connection between this type of thinking and the hikikomori, the hermits, of modern-day Japan, but the connection is there. Cognitive distortions cause us to interpret events in the worst possible way and prevent us from being resilient. Everyone will have bad experiences, but having confidence and behaving with it allows us to keep moving and turn bad circumstances into good ones. Examples from the hikikomori suggest that many of these individuals dealt with anxiety, embarrassment, bullying, or other socially isolating experiences at work. But rather than being able to overcome these circumstances, they retreated unto themselves.

The worth thing that someone dealing with anxiety and cognitive distortions can do is to withdraw from the world. Although it may be natural for someone who feels that they are being attacked or isolated from others to withdraw, all this does is reinforce their perception that the world is a dangerous, hostile place. In other words, if someone is bullied and decides to never leave the house again, all that does is confirm that underlying cognitive distortion that things are always bad, will always be bad, and are much worse than they really are. In this case, the cognitive distortions that such a person is using are global labeling and magnifying, in addition to some others. Once such a person has developed an awareness of these cognitive distortions and has learned to be mindful and recognize when they are having them, they can start to take steps toward building their self-esteem. As the reader will see in Confidence Changed My Life, building self-esteem in conjunction with mindfulness of cognitive distortions can really be what is needed to pull even the least confident person out of their hole.

We call this type of negative thinking "cognitive distortions" because that is precisely what they are: distortions. The best way to think of it is perhaps to imagine that there is objective truth in the events that unfold and that the person with the cognitive distortion is not actually seeing the truth. They are seeing a distorted picture of events, distortions that are closely tied to their own anxiety and lack of self-esteem. Although being anxious does not necessarily mean that one lacks self-esteem, when these two occur together the result can be difficult to overcome.

In Confidence Changed My Life, the steps of building confidence will be explored, beginning with understanding anxiety, cognitive distortions, and related issues, and ending with a discussion of tips the reader can follow to build their self-confidence. There are many things that impact self-confidence with anxiety being only one of those. Some individuals have issues with confidence or self-esteem because of traumatic events or poor family circumstances. Although some individuals have more to overcome than others, understanding that any circumstance can be overcome is important in changing your life through confidence.

What is confidence? Confidence can be defined as a consciousness of one's own abilities or a sense that a particular outcome will be favorable. Confidence can also be defined as a sense that a prediction or hypothesis is correct or the best. Confidence comes from the Latin word fidere which meant to rely upon, trust, or put confidence in. It is related to the Latin word fides, which means to have faith. Individuals with confidence trust in their own abilities and have faith that their beliefs are correct. Certainly, individuals can be overconfident or delusional in their confidence, but for those lacking confidence altogether being overconfident is not something they need to be particularly worried about.

Many people who lack confidence have anxiety issues but do not know it. In the first chapter, we explore anxiety, providing the reader with a working definition and an idea of the common signs and symptoms of anxiety. Anxiety is very common, with millions of people worldwide being treated for this condition. In the United States, the condition of having enduring anxiety is known as Generalized Anxiety Disorder and how this is diagnosed will be explained.

Social anxiety is particularly devastating because it leaves sufferers feeling isolated and alone. But being isolated and alone are not the only impacts of anxiety. Anxiety can impact memory, can cause feelings of inadequacy, is associated, as we have seen, with cognitive distortions and other negative thinking, and can cause fear. In the fourth chapter, these, and other impacts of anxiety on the daily lives of those who lack confidence will be explored.

The inferiority complex is an exaggerated sense that one fails to measure up to the same standards that others meet. This complex is associated with uncertainty about oneself and the world, a lack of confidence, and a pessimistic attitude. Although the idea of the inferiority complex was noted by Freud, the first true psychoanalyst, it would be his successors who took up the idea and explored all the ways that a sense of inferiority can motivate us to achieve (or fail to). Indeed, psychoanalysts have proposed that infants naturally have a sense of inferiority and the subconscious desire to overcome it is a primary motivator for development. But there are a number of reasons why certain people may not be able to overcome an inferiority complex. These reasons, as well as signs of an inferiority complex, will be explored in the second chapter.

The impacts of anxiety are not merely psychological. Anxiety, like other conditions of the brain, can have a powerful impact on the body. Indeed, for many people with anxiety, the only symptom that alerts them to their angst is a sense of physical discomfort. These so-called psychosomatic symptoms, though not tied to actual physical illness can be drastic. They are caused by the hormones and neurotransmitters that are released in response to anxiety and panic. In particular, the release of cortisol in times of stress is particularly important in the impact that anxiety has. Another important effect of anxiety is related to one of the psychological effects discussed in the third chapter: fear.

Much research has been undertaken on the fear pathway in the brain. Much of the research in fear has focused on post-traumatic stress disorder, or PTSD, a condition in which sufferers feel an intense sensation of fear related to prior trauma and experience reliving the traumatic event. Such people also are hypervigilant, always on the lookout for another traumatic event.

Indeed, symptoms of PTSD - hypervigilance and intense emotional reactions to normal, everyday events - are similar to the sort of symptoms that people with severe social anxiety face. Anxious people often deal with personalization, magnification, catastrophizing, and other cognitive distortions that only intensify their anxiety and infuse fear and panic in everyday situations. The fear pathway is important in the condition of post-traumatic stress disorder, but this pathway, traveling through an area of the brain called the amygdala, is also important in other conditions that cause fear and angst. In the fourth chapter, these and other physical implications of anxiety will be explored as a precursor to understanding how overcoming anxiety and gaining confidence can be life-changing.

Negative thinking is so important in the subject of confidence that it is the subject of the fifth chapter. We have seen how magnifying, personalizing, and catastrophizing can create an endless cycle of anxiety and depression that can derail an otherwise normal life. But these are not the only cognitive distortions that anxious men and women or those interested in building confidence have to be on the look pout for. Black and white thinking, the fallacy of control, magical thinking, and many others are just as common and just as important. Understanding these cognitive distortions can help the person lacking confidence get their life back.

If you are suffering from an anxiety disorder, you probably understand that anxiety frequently has triggers that make it worse. Just as the person with obsessive-compulsive disorder can have a trigger or the person with a phobia has that feared object that sets them off, so too do anxious people have triggers (and have a need for understanding them). It is important to understand triggers because it plays a role in the mindfulness that will be used to overcome angst and gain confidence. Anxiety triggers and coping skills are the subjects of the sixth chapter.

For many people, anxiety is not something that can be overcome on one's own. For some people, recognizing cognitive distortions and redirecting one's thoughts does the trick. For others, building self-confidence by learning what one is good at and pursuing it is helpful. Many people use coping skills to manage their negative thinking and worries. Others benefit from well-studied treatment modalities like group therapy, individual therapy, and/or medication. These and other treatment modalities will also be discussed in the sixth chapter.

Self-esteem is something that many people take for granted. It is also a thing that many people do not understand. Some people believe that self-esteem is something that you are born with or not, but many people actually work hard to overcome a lack of self-esteem in their lives. In chapter seven, the importance of self-esteem and its relationship with confidence will be explored. The topic of codependency and the manner in which it is closely related to self-esteem and confidence will also be addressed.

Understanding the importance of self-esteem can only get you so far. Many people faced with low self-esteem and low self-confidence are faced with the question of how do they imbue these qualities into their lives. In the eighth chapter, tips for building self-esteem and self-confidence will be examined. An important part of self-esteem is understanding one's own self-worth, which can be difficult in a day and age where we are constantly bombarded with information and images of and about others who seem to be doing much better than ourselves. It is natural as a human being to compare oneself to others as it reinforces the idea that we are part of a group and have a role in the group. Though that may be true, building self-esteem is sometimes as simple as spending less time comparing oneself to others and recognizing that we all, as human beings, are on a personal journey.

Sometimes that persona journey can land you in a rut. Being in a rut involves lacking the energy, drive, or desire to accomplish one’s goals. By definition, a rut represents a change in a person’s normal state of motivation.

Someone who has never been motivated can hardly be described as “being in a rut” unless that rut has lasted their entire life. That being said, ruts are important to discuss because the solutions to getting out of a rut can be applied to anyone dealing with a lack of motivation, especially those with confidence issues. Indeed, though many never realize it, a lack of confidence plays an important part in the state of being in a rut. At the very least, ruts become prolonged in duration because of a lack of confidence in one’s own abilities.

An advanced understanding of skills that help in social situations is important in building confidence and behaving confidently. These are social skills that many people have to learn. In the tenth chapter, communication skills important for living confidently will be explored. These communication skills include assertive communication, although understanding the importance of non-verbal communication is also helpful.

Though the person seeking to build confidence may ignore anxiety, it is a subject that it is unwise to push to the side. For some people, admitting that they have anxiety may be difficult. They may think that they just do not like dealing with other people, are introverted, or may have another justification for why they have become socially withdrawn. The truth of the matter is, human beings are social creatures and most people are unlikely to be successful and happy if they are not able to work well with others. A necessary component of confidence is feeling confident in your interactions with others. In the last two chapters, tips on building this sort of confidence and steps to accomplish it will be discussed.

Many readers of this book may be surprised to discover how deep their lack of confidence is or that they have a persistent inferiority complex. It is not unusual to be in this predicament as there are many common reasons why someone may feel this way. Indeed, many people develop this sort of complex because of how they are perceived and treated by the outside world. One of the ideas in this book is that it is possible to change your circumstances and change your life. This can be done by making an effort to work on your self-esteem and confidence.

Confidence may be elusive for many, but it is necessary to live a happy, healthy life. Like or not, our world is becoming more interconnected every day making the ability to enter social situations with confidence an essential quality. Someone who does not understand the importance of having confidence in social situations risks becoming like the hikikomori, deep in a well of isolation without the possibility of escape. This may seem like a fate far removed from your own life, but it may not be as removed as you think. Averting this fate involves recognizing that many problems with confidence stem from anxiety, the subject where we will begin our exploration of self-confidence.

CHAPTER 1
The Role Of Anxiety

Anxiety has become a social problem. When we say social problems, we do not mean a social ill, something that represents bad behavior by a wide variety of people. What we mean is that anxiety has become an issue that millions of people in the Westernized world deal with. Anxiety has become an epidemic, impacting the quality of life and productivity of men and women of all backgrounds.

The discussion of confidence begins with anxiety. Confidence, as we have learned, refers to the ability to trust, to have faith in, one's own abilities and that things will turn out as expected. But an anxious person does not have trust, whether this trust is in their environment or in themselves. The symptoms of the anxious person reflect the reality that the world is in some ways something hostile or threatening. Although the anxious person may not be aware that they face an issue with confidence when an anxious person begins to work towards building confidence, they may find that their circumstances drastically change.

Anxiety is a sticky subject. Many people who deal with issues of mental health may be reluctant to admit that they face issues with anxiety. For many people, being anxious implies that they have a lack of self-esteem or feel low self-worth, which, though it is often the case, is something that is hard for many people to admit. Admitting that one has anxiety is like looking in the mirror knowing that the person that you see may not be to your liking.

If one were to ask the hikikomori of Japan what keeps them sequestered in the room, away from the millions of interconnected people of the outside world, they would most likely say that they do not relate to other people or that they feel safer in their own, private space. Few would admit that they are anxious or are facing issues of self-confidence. Indeed, this is part of what makes the hikikomori difficult to treat. Treating an anxious person first requires that the person to be treated admits that they have the problem.

Defining Anxiety

Most people have an image that comes to mind when they think of anxiety. A famous etching from Alexander Morison's 1840s book on anxiety shows an image of a woman with slightly disheveled hair, a furrowed brow, and suspicious eyes. She is anxious, and the way that her face has been drawn is meant to indicate that. The disheveled hair perhaps indicates that the woman's worries have caused her to neglect her appearance somewhat while the furrowed brows suggest that underlying worry itself. The suspicious eyes are a clue as to how she perceives the world and the people in it.

Indeed, Alexander Morison's book entitled the Physiognomy of Mental Diseases was designed to help the medical professional recognize the conditions contained therein. Just as a modern medical textbook has images of scabies, shingles, skin cancer, and other conditions, Alexander Morison's book had an image of anxiety, designed to alert the medical professional right away that this serious condition was the issue at hand based solely on the appearance of the subject.

So, what is anxiety? Anxiety is defined as a sense of apprehension, uneasiness, or fear. This sense is caused by uncertainty about the future. Anxiety can also refer to the state of experiencing this particular feeling. So, someone that is anxious may not merely feel a brief sensation of apprehension or worry about a situation but may have a prolonged experience of being and feeling worried. Indeed, as we shall see later, some of the unhealthy habits of the anxious person turn what may begin as a feeling into something that becomes prolonged, even enveloping the daily life of the sufferer.

The word anxiety is readily found in the root language, Latin, where *anxietas* is the equivalent word while *anxius* is the feeling. Both *anxietas* and *anxius* stem from *ango*, which means to trouble or to distress. Indeed, the anxious person is troubled or distressed by happenings in their environment, and the implication is that these distressing things should not normally cause the level of disturbance that they cause in the anxious person.

What is important to note about anxiety is that it readily morphs into something more than a mental or emotional feeling of unease. Anxious people frequently experience physical symptoms. Indeed, for many people, these physical symptoms are the only clue that they are feeling anxious. And lest one believes that physical symptoms of this nature can be easily ignored, these symptoms can be so debilitating that suffers are unable to work effectively, leave their places of employment, or go from doctor to doctor looking for an underlying cause for their discomfort.

Anxiety is one of the most common reasons that patients visit their primary care provider. Although anxious is a feeling, an emotion, it can manifest in a physical way. Indeed, most people who go to the doctor with anxiety do not state feelings of anxiousness as their reason. They generally have a physical symptom and it is left to the doctor to piece together that these symptoms are physical manifestations of anxiety. unfortunately, many patients also do not have the furrowed brow, disheveled hair, and suspicious eyes of the woman from Alexander Morison's medical handbook written more than two hundred years ago. As the reader will soon discover, anxious people are not cookie cutter.

There are many body symptoms that anxious men and women present to the doctor. Some of these symptoms include low energy, problems sleeping, stomach upset, and pain. There are also many disorders that are categorized in modern-day psychiatry as "anxiety disorders." These anxiety disorders include generalized anxiety disorder as well as Post-traumatic stress disorder, obsessive-compulsive disorder, panic disorder, and social anxiety.

There are many stressors in the world today that may be related to a rise in anxiety in the developed world. In the past, most men and women lived in communities that were populated with close family members. Today, many people live in cities where they have no family members at all. Although it is controversial to say that anxiety is caused by factors like urbanization and increased mobility, it is certainly the case that the support networks that protected people from anxiety in the past have been eroded if not removed completely. What this means is that confidence, too, has experienced an erosion.

Think about who you meet and talk to in the day. Some people may go through their entire day without having a face-to-face conversation with a loved one or family member at all. The people that they work with are effectively strangers as are the other residents in their apartment building or the people they encounter on a train. The support that comes from having family members that know you and love you are is gone for most people, undercutting part of the foundation of many people's confidences.

What this means is that confidence today is something that many people will have to work toward. It is not difficult to feel confident when you are around people who know that you are capable and are willing to support you. But how will you be motivated to achieve with confidence in a competitive world around people who you do not know and who may not be favorably disposed toward you? The modern person has to adapt to the changing face of the world today, and that may mean understanding that they are anxious, learning why they are anxious, and overcoming it.

Diagnosing Generalized Anxiety Disorder

Generalized anxiety disorder is the name for the condition associated with anxiety about places and events. This type of anxiety is distinct from a phobia which is worry or fear about a specific object, or obsessive-compulsive disorder, which involves obsessive thoughts and compulsive behaviors that are often related to a trigger. Generalized anxiety, therefore, is nonspecific, with anxious people often being triggered by everyday events or activities or by nothing at all. An anxious person may feel worried or unease most of the time or, as we have seen, they may feel a physical symptom that is related to their anxiety.

Generalized anxiety disorder, or GAD, is exceedingly common. It is estimated that about two percent of adults in the United States and Europe have symptoms of GAD.

The lifetime prevalence of GAD worldwide is about twice as high, at about four percent. Evidence from the psychological study suggests that GAD is more common in Westernized countries although the link between Westernization and mental disorders like anxiety is not well understood. Indeed, as countries adopt the accouterments of Western life studies show that anxiety disorders become more common.

Although GAD affects both women and men, it is twice as common in women as in men. There are many comorbidities associated with anxiety, several of which are mental health-related. For example, studies suggest that anxiety disorders are present in nearly 60% of people diagnosed with major depression. It is believed that nearly 20% of people with depression have generalized anxiety disorder with a lesser number having panic disorder. Depression is also common in people with a generalized anxiety disorder. Although some anxious people do not have depression severe enough for a diagnosis of major depressive disorder, many anxious people can be diagnosed with dysthymia, which is characterized by a lower level of depressing thought that is felt most of the time rather than depressive episodes. Other comorbidities associated with anxiety include substance abuse disorder, attention deficit hyperactivity disorder, and substance abuse disorder.

As a condition in the Diagnostic and Statistical Manual of Mental Disorders, or DSM, generalized anxiety disorder was introduced in 1980 with the third edition. At this time, the condition of anxiety neurosis was split into panic disorder and generalized anxiety disorder. Anxiety needed to be excessive and lasting for at least a month in order for the diagnosis of GAD to be made. With each edition of the DSM, the criteria for diagnosis have been tweaked somewhat. In the most recent edition, the DSM-5, anxiety has to be experienced more days in the week than not and it can be felt related to a wide variety of topics.

In the United States, the DSM is generally used to make a diagnosis of GAD although other counties may use the ICD-10 criteria. The criteria used in the DSM-5 to make a diagnosis of GAD include the following:

- Excessive anxiety or worry that lasts more than six months. This worry is present the majority of the time across many activities.
- Inability to manage symptoms of anxiety
- The presence of three or more of the following:
- Difficulty sleeping
- Irritable mood
- Difficulty concentrating

- Easily fatigued
- Tension in the muscles
- Restlessness
- Anxiety symptoms are dysfunctional
- Anxiety symptoms are not related to taking medication, substance, or another medical problem
- Anxiety symptoms are not better accounted for by another diagnosis, like post-traumatic stress disorder or panic disorder

The Connection Between Anxiety and Self-Esteem

Individuals who do not experience anxiety may make assumptions about self-esteem (or lack thereof) of anxious people. Although in this book anxiety is discussed as a precursor to building confidence, feelings of anxiety or depression do not automatically mean that a person is lacking in confidence. Anxious people may have social anxiety which causes them to avoid situations where they have to interact with others, a subject that will be discussed further shortly, but they make have confidence in other areas.

For example, someone who has experienced abuse, neglect, or bullying early on in their life may grow up to have anxiety, depression, or a hypersensitive personality. These individuals may be hyperaware of how they are treated by others and they may ruminate for hours after interactions that most other people easily ignore. Even psychotherapists often assume that this type of hypersensitivity stems from a lack of confidence when it is really an issue of a traumatic experience, like bullying, being manifested as hypersensitivity about how one is treated by others.

A hypersensitive individual may withdraw from others, essentially being or behaving like an introvert, but it is not necessarily because of a lack of confidence. Take the example of someone who was bullied because they were short, had a birth defect, or had something else that set them out as different from other people. This person may be hypersensitive about how others treat them and defensive, but at the same time may recognize that they are an excellent scientist, a good wife, and mother, or an all-around good person.

The point here is to establish that although anxiety and confidence are related, the presence of the first does not automatically indicate the lack of the second. The approach of this book is rather to say that the absence of the second may be a good place for the person lacking this to think about if they have the first thing. The analogy to make here is the case of someone whose clothes smell like cigarette smoke. The clothes may smell like cigarette smoke because they are a smoker, but it also may be the case that their significant other is a smoker, they live with a smoker, or they work in a cigarette factory. If this person does not want their clothes to smell like smoke, it is fair to ask, well, do you smoke? At the same time, we recognize that not everyone who smokes has clothes that smell like cigarette smoke. Yes, it is an odd analogy but it underlines the point that we need to ask people who are working on their confidence if they are anxious without assuming that at all anxious people lack confidence.

Let us return to the example of the hikikomori of Japan. Their example underscores the idea that we cannot make assumptions going in the other direction either. For example, hermits living this way lack the confidence to function in the modern world. But we have to be careful not to assume that they are all suffering from anxiety and depression. Sure, some of them likely do, but if the issue was that then the hikikomori would be easier to treat than they are proving to be. Anxiety and confidence can be connected but the connection is not as straightforward as it seems. The best way to approach the issue is to ask those interested in building their self-esteem if issues of anxiety may be playing a role in their lives.

Why is it important to ask this question? Well, the answer is simple. As readers of this book will soon discover, developing confidence can truly change lives. Books that talk about how to win friends and influence people or how to succeed in this or that without really trying, these books are really about how success in life is closely tied to social skills and the basic building block of social skills is confidence. Just as animals are said to sense fear, other people can sense a lack of confidence and, like it or not, your future can be tied to how confident you are as perceived by other people.

The Inferiority Complex

It is important to analyze how individuals view themselves and their place in the world when attempting to understand anxiety. It is also crucial to understand this when understanding confidence. Although the idea of the inferiority complex dates back to the times of Sigmund Freud, the founder of psychoanalysis, it would be later psychologists like Carl Jung and especially Alfred Adler who picked up on this idea and explored it as a basis for human motivation. These were the early years of psychoanalysis and modern-day social science. Clinicians and researchers like Freud, Jung, and Adler explored their ideas at a time when people were just beginning to understand how humans could be better understood by analyzing their thinking and their underlying motivations.

Alfred Adler, the founder of individual psychology, was a student of Sigmund Freud, but his beliefs departed from his predecessor's somewhat. While Freud believed that human beings were primarily motivated by libido and aggression, Alder saw human motivation as being purposive. That is, human actions were tied to an individual understanding of the world, which could be based on various societal factors. But an important part of Alfred Adler's psychoanalytic theory was the idea of the inferiority complex. Adler believed that this sense of inferiority naturally existed during infancy when the child feels a sense of smallness and dependence upon the adult.

This idea of inferiority as a primary motivation that existed during infancy departed from Freud and other psychologists who believed that infants were naturally narcissistic and they became less so through a process of normal development. Instead of focusing on narcissism with its associated libidinous (sexual) and aggressive drives, Adler focused on inferiority with overcoming this inferiority being a driving force for development.

The reason why it is important to understand the inferiority complex early on in the discussion of confidence (and anxiety) is to present the idea that a sense of being less than others is not necessarily abnormal. In modern-day America, people are expected to be confident and outgoing, and it is taken for granted that many people (if not most) are not naturally confident and have to work towards reaching this state.

Although Adler believed that an inferiority complex was the natural state of affairs for the infant, he thought that this complex, rather than being overcome in a normal way, could be exaggerated and persistent. Factors that could cause an adult to continue to have a severe inferiority complex include a physical handicap or disability, abuse or neglect, or environmental factors (stressors). Adults also can naturally have an inferiority complex, but this so-called secondary inferiority complex was the result of being a perfectionist and being pessimistic about life.

It is interesting here to return to the hikikomori and ponder if their circumstances could be related to an inferiority complex. Even if we say that many of the hikikomori do not suffer from a mental condition like anxiety or depression that traps them in their hermitic state, this does not exclude the possibility that societal factors have caused them to have an exaggerated and persistent sense of inferiority. As we will see, the solution, in this case, would be to invest in activities that build confidence so that the person who feels inferior, whether they are conscious of it or not, has a well of self-esteem to draw from as they go out and face the world.

Social Anxiety

Social anxiety is a phenomenon that has attracted much attention in recent years. At its most basic, social anxiety refers to unease or fear around common social situations, though this definition does not fully capture how distressing this type of anxiety can be. Men and women with social anxiety may ruminate for hours on simple activities like going to the post office to mail a package or going for a routine doctor's visit because of their feelings. Social anxiety is related to generalized anxiety though it is tied specifically to fear around social activity. Anxious people can have social anxiety in addition to having anxiety about other things.

Social anxiety is also known as social phobia, which underscores what this condition is really about. People that have phobias experience excessive fear and worry about a particular situation (or object), and in the case of social phobia, that situation is a social one. An important component of phobias is that the person with the phobia worries about the object or situation even when they are not exposed to it. So, a person who has a fear of clowns may worry that they may run into a clown even though there is no logical reason to expect this. In much the same way, people with social phobia or social anxiety have fears that seem out of proportion to the reality of the situation.

Although it may seem easy to make the assumption that people like this have been traumatized by experience, as is the case in other anxiety disorders (and mental conditions in general) there are other factors that play a role, like genetics. Some people simply have a genetic predisposition towards developing anxiety disorders and this includes social phobia. It is also important to recognize mental health the idea of protective factors. Some individuals may be at risk for developing anxiety disorders but may be protected from expressing these characteristics by a positive, supportive family environment, a comfortable economic situation, and similar protective factors.

CHAPTER 2

Overcoming an Inferiority Complex

The inferiority complex is an interesting subject for a number of reasons. One is the idea from psychoanalysis that all human beings are born with an inferiority complex. Another reason is the burgeoning concept that the problem of the inferiority complex is worsening with millions of people dealing with this underlying problem in ways that perhaps were not true in the past. We all can admit that our society has changed in drastic ways in the last fifty years, but it is not always easy to understand how people may have changed psychologically.

What do we mean by this? It is easy to see that the world is superficially very different than it was in the sixties and seventies. Most people these days not only have a personal computer with access to the internet but mobile phones that allow them to communicate instantly. Most people in the developed world have access to satellite television where they are exposed to cable news, reality television, and other forms of programming. Men and women are delaying having children if they choose to have them at all, and there has been a measure of role reversal for the sexes with some men choosing to stay home and parent and many women choosing highly competitive jobs.

What does any of this have to do with the inferiority complex? Well, the fact of the matter is that our society has become more communicative, more visual, arguably more materialistic, and certainly more competitive. It has been argued that looks are more important now than ever before with most people having social media accounts where pictures of themselves are prominently displayed. In fact, employers often look at social media accounts when they are deciding to hire someone. In some countries, prospective candidates are expected to provide their picture along with their resume.

Although this discussion is not meant to suggest that people should have an inferiority complex because of these conditions, it is not hard to understand why they do. If we get into the habit of comparing ourselves to others as our society primes us to do, it is not too surprising that we may find ourselves wanting. There will always be someone out there who is better looking than we are, smarter, better educated, married to a more attractive spouse, younger, or wealthier. If these labels are important to us, and many of them are, we will generally find ourselves wanting.

But what is important to recognize here is that no one is perfect. There will always be someone who is superior to you in something, no matter how incredible you are. Stephen King is an accomplished writer, but he certainly is an inferior cook to Wolfgang Puck. Luciano Pavarotti may be one of the greatest tenors of modern times, but he is certainly an inferior dancer, Rubik's cube player, or marathon runner than millions of others.

One of the themes of this chapter is that though inferiority complexes may be normal (and increasingly more common), being a perfectionist and wanting to be the best at everything will only heighten the sense that you can never be that the best and that you are a failure. This perfectionism, though it may drive some people, usually becomes a problem eventually. And to the person with low self-confidence, it is nothing less than poison. We begin our discussion of inferiority complexes (and overcoming them) by taking a look at the root causes.

Causes of an Inferiority Complex

If we believe the psychoanalysts, everyone is born with an inferiority complex that they overcome through the normal process of development. An inferiority complex, however, can become a dysfunctional part of an adult existence when certain factors because what is essentially a distorted sense that one is less than others to continue to be a factor as an adult. Here, we will explore the following causes for this state of affairs:

- Presence of a physical handicap or disability
- History of abuse or neglect during childhood
- Environmental and social stressors
- Perfectionist approach to life (and a pessimistic attitude)

One of the assumptions that underlie the idea that the inferiority complex eventually dissipates is this idea that people are not actually inferior to others so they have no reason to believe this. In other words, the child is weak and dependent on the adult, according to Adler, but as they develop autonomy and a normal sense of self, they should no longer be inferior to others. This happens as a child progresses into adulthood. But what if a particular circumstance causes someone to continue to feel that they are inferior?

This is where a physical handicap or disability becomes a cause of an inferiority complex. Individuals with a handicap may not only have a subconscious belief that they are less than other people because they are different, but they may also be exposed to bullying or abuse that reinforces this idea that they are different from others. Individuals who are not able to draw from a store of self-confidence to overcome this situation may continue to have an inferiority complex into their adult life.

This cause of an inferiority complex can be compounded by the presence of one of the other causes, which will be discussed shortly.

A history of abuse or neglect is tied to several issues that can surface in adult life. For example, people that have been abused or neglected may be more likely to develop anxiety and depression in adulthood. Such persons may also be at increased risk for developing a personality disorder or issues that we commonly associate with personality disorders such as codependency. The abused person is not to blame for what happened to them, an idea that it often takes a therapist or other health professional to impart. Individuals in these circumstances can benefit from exercises that build their self-esteem, helping them to understand that they are not their past experiences.

Stressors in home life or social factors can also be a major cause of an inferiority complex. For example, people that are exposed to discrimination or another mistreatment early on in life can internalize negative beliefs about themselves. Indeed, such persons may not be conscious that they dislike themselves and that this comes from the society around them. This is almost a type of Stockholm Syndrome where the person identifies with those who are part of the system of abuse rather than loving themselves. Learning to love and value oneself is an important way to overcome this cause of an inferiority complex.

It may be hard to picture, but perfectionists frequently have a pessimistic view of the world. Though we may be inclined to think of perfectionists as people who are "perfect" and expect others to be the same as they are, perfectionists are often imperfect people who are constantly faced with their own imperfections, which makes them miserable. They may project their low sense of self onto others by judging them harshly and being intolerant, a clue that one has an inferiority complex that will be explored further below.

Signs that Someone Has an Inferiority Complex

People who feel inferior do not wear a scarlet letter across their breasts to indicate this. They look just like everyone else. Indeed, people who seem to have perfect lives may suffer from an inferior complex even more so than the person who is on their own and living on the street. We cannot make assumptions about others. We also have to beware to make assumptions about ourselves. You may seem to the outside world to be "normal" and "successful" but might be dealing with issues beyond your control, issues that affect your confidence. Below is a list of signs that may help you to determine if an inferiority complex may be a factor in your life.

- You are highly judgmental of others (criticizing others and finding fault with them)
- You have intense feelings of guilt, shame, and envy
- You have a false, inflated sense of superiority (trying hard to hide one's own inferiority)
- You are prone to passive behaviors and overall procrastination
- You feeling a strong need to please others and fit into the crowd
- You perceive others as a threat to yourself
- You are highly sensitive to criticism
- You withdraw from society or engage in attention-seeking behaviors
- You comparing yourself to others to your disadvantage

Highly Judgmental of Others

Unfortunately, many people judge others harshly. Although we may be tempted to say that social media has made this more of a problem in our modern society, the reality is that this is always been something that societies have had to deal with. Indeed, some religions focus on preaching tolerance, love, and acceptance to help men and women to overcome what seems to be an ever-present part of the human experience. Those who are highly judgmental engage in criticizing others and finding fault with them. What such people do not often understand is that they really find fault with themselves and project this onto others subconsciously. A confident person does not need to judge others harshly or be cruel to them.

Feelings of Guilt, Shame, and Envy

Related to being highly judgmental of others is the trifecta of guilt, shame, and envy. Guilt and shame are caused by feelings that one has performed wrongly in a particular situation as well as a sense that there is something intrinsically wrong with yourself that causes you to behave that way. Someone who is ashamed, instead of judging others harshly, judges themselves harshly. Indeed, an important part of overcoming guilt and shame is so-called radical acceptance in which one accepts all aspects of themselves no matter how hard it may be. Envy is a desire to have what others have, and it also stems from underlying dissatisfaction with oneself.

False, Inflated Sense of Superiority

It is not difficult to understand why people with an inferiority complex develop an inflated sense of superiority. This situation is not altogether different from that of the narcissist who acts superior and entitled, leading them to abuse others, but really feels a deep sense of inadequacy and needs the validation of others. People with an inferiority complex can be superior and grandiose because they are trying hard to hide their own sense of inferiority.

Prone to Passive Behaviors and Overall Procrastination

This is a sign of an inferiority complex that some may not have suspected. Those who have an inferiority complex may be generally passive and procrastinators. Such individuals behave this way because they are avoiding situations and people that cause them to be reminded of their feelings of inferiority. Think about procrastination. Why do we procrastinate? Because we do not want to deal with the specific thing that we need to deal with, right? Well, in the case of people who feel inferior, they do not want to be faced with their inferiority because of the feelings it engenders – anger, self-loathing, sadness – and so they avoid it altogether.

Feeling a Strong Need to Please Others and Fit into the Crowd

People who are confident feel comfortable being alone. Indeed, learning to be okay on one's own is actually one of the steps that are advised for people who have been in abusive relationships, have codependency issues, or have other problems with abuse or mental health. Although it may seem natural to want the approval of others, this need can be unhealthy. Indeed, it is associated with people who are codependent and end up with individuals who are narcissists, manipulators, or otherwise abusive. If you desire to be confident, you have to stop worrying about fitting in.

Perceiving Others as a Threat to Oneself

Perceiving others (and the world itself) as threatening is a sign of an inferiority complex that is closely tied to several of the causes of this state. People that have been abused or neglected can perceive the world as threatening because, in their experience, it is. A child who has been abused by a loved one never knows what it feels like to trust others because they were hurt by the person closest to them. A child who has been neglected does not have the experience of a parent who was able to make them feel safe and secure so they grow up to see the world as an inherently unsafe, insecure place. One way for these people to become confident and achieve the success that comes with it is to do some reality testing. Is the world really as threatening as they think it is? That is the question they answer through experience.

Highly Sensitive to Criticism

Most people can be sensitive to criticism by others. This is not inherently abnormal. But someone who allows their entire sense of self to be destroyed by the criticism that they get from others has an inferiority complex. If someone criticizes you about something and you know it is not true, then why should it bother you? If this criticism bothers you greatly, it is either because you subconsciously suspect that it may be true or you are afraid that others may believe it to be true and you desperately want their approval.

Withdrawing from Society or Engaging in Attention Seeking Behaviors

This brings us back to the hikikomori, the hermits, of modern-day Japan. Withdrawing from society completely is, we have to admit, a highly abnormal behavior. Human beings are naturally social creatures, like other primates, and they commonly form social groups that serve several purposes. Therefore, abandoning society altogether is a sign of a deep underlying problem. Conversely, individuals with an inferiority complex can engage in attention-seeking behaviors. Indeed, it can even be argued that withdrawing from society is a type of attention-seeking behavior.

Comparing Yourself to Others to Your Disadvantage

Comparing oneself to others and finding oneself lacking is a textbook indication of an inferiority complex. Although it is common, especially in this day and age, to compare ourselves to those around us, we do not necessarily have to develop a low opinion of ourselves as a result. For example, we may observe that someone is taller than us, but does that mean that we have to hate that we are short? As short as you are, there is sure to be someone shorter out there who is not bothered about it. Learning not to compare ourselves to others may be difficult in a time where "keeping up with the Jones's" seems normal, but it may be necessary if we are serious about developing our own sense of self-worth.

You may be examining these signs and noticing yourself surprised at how many of these apply to you. This is nothing to be alarmed about. As we have seen, there are many reasons why people develop an inferiority complex. Other than developmental or familial factors, social factors can also lead to this. For example, people of a particular gender or members of minority groups may deal with this because of how they are perceived and treated in society. The existence of this inferiority complex, therefore, is through no fault of your own. What you must-do if you have one is to decide that society is unlikely to change to accommodate you. You are the one who needs to change and this book is designed to help you do just that.

CHAPTER 3
The Ways Anxiety Impacts Your Daily Life

Many anxious people are unaware that what they are feeling is actually anxiety. We associate being anxious with worrying over trivial things, being hypersensitive, and fearing things that most people would not be afraid of. Although there is some truth in these assumptions about anxiety, as we have seen from our review of the symptoms needed to make a diagnosis of GAD, we have also seen that anxiety can present with physical symptoms that can be very unpleasant for the sufferer and cause dysfunction. Indeed, although anxiety is one of the primary reasons why patients visit their primary care doctor, they infrequently report that they are feeling anxious and it is left to the clinician to recognize the signs.

There are many reasons why it is important to discuss anxiety effects in the context of a discussion of building confidence. Many people may recognize that a lack of confidence and self-esteem is an issue in their lives, but they may not recognize that they may also be dealing with anxiety and that this is also impacting their ability to live confidently. By discussing the ways in which anxiety affects life, the reader is equipped to understand how their life has been changed by their anxiety and also begin to imagine how their life will be changed once anxiety has been swept away.

Needless to say, anxiety can affect the lives of the anxious person in many ways. Some of these impacts of anxiety are controversial and still being studied. For example, research from the last 10-15 years has suggested that there is a link between the presence of high anxiety levels and the development of irritable bowel syndrome, or IBS.

Gastrointestinal problems are one of the most common signs of an anxiety disorder, and the task of teasing out what is a physical illness and what is an anxiety symptom can be trying for the clinician.

Anxiety has been shown to be associated with a host of other conditions. A link between anxiety and respiratory diseases, heart disease, chronic fatigue, and pain syndromes has been demonstrated. Indeed, anxiety has been shown to be associated with a condition known as somatic symptom disorder in which the individual feels pain, weakness, dizziness, or nausea that has no known physical cause. In this chapter, we focus not on the medical conditions associated with anxiety but on some of the discrete impacts that anxiety has on the body. These areas of impact include the following:

- Memory

- Feelings of Inadequacy
- Negative Thinking
- Fear

Why does anxiety impact the body? Anxiety has such a powerful effect on the body because the anxious state is associated with the presence of hormones in the body and neurotransmitters in the brain. Also, experiences or memories that are associated with anxiety have been found to travel through a region of the brain known as the amygdala. As we will see shortly, the amygdala is an area that is associated with memories or images that have a fear component. The presence of amygdala activation is also associated with a physiological response to stress, a subject that will be explored in more detail in the next chapter.

Memory

It is easy to take memory for granted. Someone tells us their name and we remember it. We remember the "SAT words" that we read in books and occasionally use these words in sentences. We remember the names of our distant relatives and of the spouses of our favorite actors on television. But when one suffers from anxiety or depression, memory can be one of the first areas to be impacted. Anxious people may have problems recalling common things, a symptom that can be directly related to the tendency to ruminate about things and to be a heightened state of fear.

Indeed, fear, a subject that will be discussed separately shortly, is an important area to address when thinking of the memory problems that anxious people face. The heightened sense of fear that anxious people face is both a cause of anxiety and a symptom of it. As we have seen, this state is associated with memory problems. Although there are several reasons why anxious people might have problems with memory, research has shown that being anxious can cause lasting damage to the cells of the hippocampus, an area associated with learning and memory. Anxiety can lead to early memory decline, a sign that is otherwise associated with aging in the elderly.

Feelings of Inadequacy

Anxious people can feel inadequate, even if they are not completely conscious of it. They may not feel that they are good enough to be in a relationship with the people around them or that they are unqualified for their job. These feelings of inadequacy can lead to pessimistic thoughts and fear. Because such people tend to be pessimistic, to begin with, inadequacy becomes part of a cycle of dysfunctional thoughts and behaviors. Part of dealing with these feelings of inadequacy can involve treating the anxiety itself, although developing skills like learning not to compare yourself to others is also important.

Negative Thinking

As a human being, it is critical to be able to perceive danger in order to protect oneself, but anxious people are always in a state of heightened alertness. This causes them not only to sense danger in settings where there is none but to interpret events in the worse possible way. For example, something as simple as a disagreement with a coworker can turn into fears that a job will be lost and anger or vindictive behavior directed at the person the argument is with. Negative thinking is very common in anxiety and it is closely tied to lack of self-esteem and a negative world view.

Fear

Humans need fear. As we touched on earlier, fear allows human beings to be sensitive to danger and engage in behaviors designed to protect themselves. For example, even a small child knows to avoid walking near a precipice because it has a fear that it will fall into it. This fear is protective as it prevents the child, or whoever else, from engaging in behaviors that are inherently threatening to themselves. But anxious people feel fear in situations where fear is not a normal response. They may feel fear around social engagements or around objects commonly found in their environment (phobias). Fear about ordinary things activates the stress response in the body (and brain), a problematic state of affairs that leads to a host of other problems.

CHAPTER 4

The Ways Anxiety Affects Your Body

Stress is the mediating factor in anxiety's impacts on the brain. Stress is how our body responds to demands or threats. Stress is not necessarily a bad thing, but prolonged periods of stress are associated with a host of problems. Chronic stress can cause changes to your body's composition, can increase your likelihood of heart disease and other illnesses, can reduce your life expectancy and quality of life, and have many other effects.

When a person is under stress, their sympathetic nervous system sends a signal to an area in the brain called the hypothalamus. The hypothalamus then releases a hormone called cortisol-releasing hormone, or CRH. CRH travels to the pituitary gland where it triggers the release of adrenocorticotropic hormone or ACTH. The adrenal cortex is stimulated by ACTH to release cortisol, the primary hormone released in response to stress. Cortisol has many effects on the body of which two of the more important are to increase blood sugar and to increase blood pressure.

Cortisol is not the only hormone that plays a role in this sympathetic nervous system stress response. In this state, the adrenal glands are triggered to release epinephrine and norepinephrine. These chemicals have important effects on the body, too, especially as regards the cardiovascular system. Some readers may be familiar with the Epi-pen that people who are in shock due to an allergy receive to save their lives. Shock in this context happens in response to the body's exposure to a substance, which triggers a drop-in blood pressure among other things. Epinephrine is given to raise the blood pressure of those in this allergic shock and prevent them from experiencing organ failure and eventually death.

Cortisol Release and Stress

The long-term effects of stress on the body are, as we have seen, related to the chemicals that the body releases in response to stress. Stress can affect the heart, the gastrointestinal tract, the skin, the lungs, and the liver, to name a few. Stress impacts the heart by increasing blood pressure and heart rate. This happens because the body is trying to increase blood flow as it believes that it is in a situation where it has to defend itself. Stress also increases cholesterol levels, which can lead, long-term, to cardiovascular disease. People under prolonged stress are at increased risk of stroke, heart attack, and heart failure.

Before you discount the role that stress has on the body, it is important to mention that research suggests that stress from work and home is associated with a 50% increased chance of coronary artery disease. Related to the impact that cortisol and stress have on the heart is the impact on the lungs. The lungs respond to stress by increasing respiratory rate or breathing. This causes hyperventilation, which can lead to panic attacks and trigger asthma attacks. Stress is also linked to chronic obstructive pulmonary disease or COPD.

Stress impacts the gastrointestinal system, which we touched on briefly previously. Stress can trigger overeating. People who are stressed in response to situations where they are not actually in danger tend to overeat. This is very unhealthy as stress causes the release of cortisol, which increases blood sugar. The result is that people who are stressed and who are under eat can become insulin resistant and develop type 2 diabetes. Obesity is very common in the Western world, with rates of 20% - 40% being common in North America.

Many people are unaware that stress can impact the skin. Stress increases the risk of eczema and psoriasis, two common and unpleasant skin conditions. These conditions cause the development of scaly patches, which can flare up in direct relationship to stress. Psoriasis is considered a serious global problem, which affects over 100 million people around the globe.

The endocrine system is one of the body's systems that is most heavily influenced by stress. This is because the endocrine system plays a role in metabolism and energy, and since we need the energy to be able to fight and survive when we are threatened this system is primed to respond to rises in cortisol levels. The release of cortisol causes an increase in blood sugar levels, as we have seen. Blood sugar levels increase in order to provide the body's muscles with energy for fight or flight.

The problem with prolonged stress as is seen in anxiety is that it leads to prolonged increases in blood sugar levels. Type II diabetes results from prolonged hyperglycemia because the body becomes resistant to insulin. Insulin's job is to stimulate the cells to uptake glucose, a type of sugar, into the cells. But if your blood always has high levels of glucose then your body is always being exposed to insulin, which it eventually becomes resistant to. This leads to type II diabetes, a condition associated with significant morbidity.

The Fear Pathway in the Brain

Anxiety, by definition, is the feeling of worry or fear in response to every day, non-specific situations. As opposed to specific phobias, where people feel anxiety about a particular object that they are afraid of, in generalized anxiety disorder men and women worry about a wide variety of things in their daily lives. But what is so important about a fear that we need to point it out as a mitigating factor of the effects of anxiety. Well, fear is important because memories associated with fear activate special areas of the brain, but fear becomes part of a vicious cycle of stress and anxiety that essentially becomes a hole that the sufferer has to dig themselves out of. In other words, when you experience fear in response to normal, everyday events, you become primed to experience fear even more, which makes the anxiety and stress worse.

But what is interesting about fear is the role that it plays in the brain. Studies of people with post-traumatic stress disorder, or PTSD, have revealed that memories associated with fear activate a region of the brain called the amygdala. Although this may seem like a useless fact, people with PTSD who activate their amygdala experience such unpleasant symptoms as hypersensitivity, hypervigilance, problems sleeping, and stress.

We can think about it with the following example. Someone who has been in war and, as a result, has developed PTSD may be triggered to experience their PTSD symptoms based on loud noises, crowds of people, enclosed spaces, or other things. So, when a person with PTSD goes to a concert or other loud event, their experiences, and memories of that event travel through the amygdala, the fear center, rather than the normal memory pathways of the brain. That means that when they recall that event, they will experience fear even though there was nothing frightening about that experience. Of course, the person with PTSD also will have experienced PTSD symptoms during the event.

What all this means in the overall context of building confidence is that anxiety is not just something that can give you a stomach ache or otherwise make you uncomfortable. Untreated anxiety can damage the body's systems, cause you to develop diabetes, cause you to become obese, and shorten your lifespan. In the long run, this will just give you something else to be anxious and depressed out. If you want to change your life, leading the happy life that you know you deserve, it becomes important to overcome anxiety and work on building up your self-esteem.

CHAPTER 5

Cognitive Distortions in Anxiety

Cognitive distortions serve the role of reinforcing the negative perceptions and life outcomes associated with anxiety. This means that if you are not able to recognize and change your cognitive distortions then you are unlikely to be able to gain the confidence that will allow you to change your life. Through cognitive distortions, anxious people create a world that is dangerous and hostile, literally creating it by interpreting events such that they always fit their perceptions.

Psychotherapists typically tell their patients that have cognitive distortions that no matter what experiences they have, even good ones, they will always interpret things as going negatively because of their negative thinking. It does not matter what the reality is; the distorted thinking of the anxious or depressed person causes them to see things as something other than what they really are. This is essentially what a cognitive distortion is: a way of thinking that leads a person to interpret events in an untrue, exaggerated or otherwise negative way.

How Distorted Thinking Impacts Our Daily Lives

Cognitive distortions impact the lives of millions of people. Indeed, there are many people who will reach the end of their life not realizing that they have perceived the world in a distorted way. This is why you have made the right step in reading this particular book. In this chapter specifically, you will learn the sorts of distorted thinking patterns that prevent people from being confident by causing them to always view other people and the world itself with fear.

It would be ridiculous to imply that there are not bad people out there. There are. There are people who may want to harm you, embarrass you, or belittle you. But what good does it do you to perceive everyone you meet as having these designs? It does no good at all. All it serves is to make you fearful and stressed, and we have already seen the effects that stress has on life, the body, and the brain. Here we will review the major types of distortions that can derail your life. The major type of cognitive distortions is listed below. Following the list, each one will be described briefly to help you recognize it and the role it may be playing in your thinking.

- Black and White Thinking
- Filtering
- Magnifying
- Minimizing
- Personalizing
- Overgeneralization

- Catastrophizing
- Jumping to Conclusions
- Fallacy of Control
- Fallacy of Fairness
- Emotional Reasoning
- Blaming
- Shoulds
- Global Labeling
- Magical Thinking

Black and White Thinking

Black and white thinking is also known as polarized thinking. Just as the name implies, a person with polarized thinking sees life as being all on one side or on the other. People are either all good or all bad. If a person is not completely perfect then they are a loser, a black and white ideal that such people apply to themselves. It is not difficult to see why this is a problem. Life exists in shades of gray. We may fail at something and still be a decent person. We may say something untoward to our parents on one occasion, but that does not make us an evil person. Recognizing that things are not all one way or all another is important in order to see the world as it really is.

Filtering

Filtering is one of the more common types of cognitive distortions. People who are anxious and depressed do this so frequently that they do not realize they do it. In filtering, we exclude the positive things and focus on the negative things, even to the point of magnifying the negative. For example, someone on the way to work has road rage and yells an expletive at you and so you decide that human beings are evil and what's the point of working towards anything because the world is a horrible place. But you forget the elderly woman who was kind to you at the coffee shop or the coworker who told you that day that you are the hardest working person they have met and to keep up the good work. People who filter completely ignore all the good things and focus solely on one or two bad things. It is hard to be happy and confident thinking like this.

Magnifying

Magnifying is huge, too. Indeed, magnifying plays a role in some of the other cognitive distortions. Magnifying is when we see things as being much worse than they really are. It really is a way of viewing the world in an unrealistic light. So, a bad run-in with a coworker leads you to pack up your personal things at work because there is no way you can continue to work in a place where you do not get along with anyone so you might as well just leave now. What have you done here? You have just taken a bad encounter that most people have at work and decided to leave your job over it. You blew things completely out of proportion.

Minimizing

Minimizing is similar to magnifying except that instead of blowing things out of proportion they reduce them to the point of insignificance. So, using the example that we mentioned previously, someone who had a bad encounter with a coworker will decide to leave their job, completely minimizing the five years of hard work and the recognition they have received for that work. They have minimized the good things in their life because their brain focuses solely on the bad.

Personalizing

Personalizing is an interesting one because it is not confined to individuals that suffer from anxiety and depression. Many people personalize situations and are entirely unaware that they do it. In personalizing, the individual attaches personal meaning to events that really have nothing to do with them. So, a person who comes to work and sees that a particular coworker does not greet them will think that they are mad about something they have done and have decided as a result to ignore them or be rude to them. The reality is, perhaps the coworker did not see them, is not feeling well, or is having a bad day. Not everything that happens around you has to do with you.

Overgeneralization

We have touched on overgeneralization a bit, mostly because this, too, is related to the other distortions. Overgeneralization involves taking something that happens in one instance and applying it to everything. So, just because you dealt with some road rage this morning at the hands of someone who was not being nice to you, does that mean that everyone is horrible all the time? That is clearly an overgeneralization. Sensitive people tend to overgeneralize, which is understandable, but it is an impediment to being happy and confident.

Catastrophizing

People who catastrophize believe that the world is ending over the simple things that happen in the day. So, for example, if someone is running a little bit late to work because of traffic, this person will immediately think that they are going to lose their job, their wife will leave them, and they will be alone for the rest of their lives. This is a strange conclusion to reach just because you are running a little late. For all you know, the traffic will clear and you may be on time. Or perhaps your boss is behind you in traffic and will be even later than you are. Even if you are late, what are the odds you will be fired for being late once? You have catastrophized and you need to stop!

Jumping to Conclusions

We all jump to conclusions and most of us do not realize how distorted and dysfunctional this behavior is. When we jump to conclusions, we add two and two and get seven. We reach a conclusion that has little or nothing to do with what actually happened. For example, if someone steps on your foot as you are sitting in a waiting room does that mean they did it on purpose because they are mad about a comment you left on someone's social media page? If the person at the coffee shop spells your name wrong on the cup that they hand you is it because they dislike you personally? No. You have jumped to a conclusion that has sent you on a wild goose chase of anger and anxiety.

Fallacy of Control

The fallacy of control is something that we see frequently in those who have anxiety, depression, or other mental conditions. The fallacy of control is when we think that events or either entirely outside of our control or, conversely, specifically under our control. When we see events outside of our control, this is called external control and it is dysfunctional because it leads us to perceive ourselves as powerless victims. When we have internal control, we will tend to personalize events and see everything as having something to do with us. Both circumstances worsen anxiety and derail confidence.

Fallacy of Fairness

The fallacy of fairness is a tricky one because some cultural or religious beliefs can reinforce it. The fallacy of fairness is the belief that the world is meant to be "fair" or "just" and it causes people to interpret events based on this paradigm. This type of thinking can be dysfunctional because it leads people to become angry or depressed when things happen that they see as unfair or unjust. This can lead people to feel that they are being unjustly persecuted or targeted, which can reinforce their anxiety and isolate them.

Emotional Reasoning

In emotional reasoning, someone believes that how they feel about things is the way that they are. An emotional sensation of anger or fear is not something internal, that is, reflecting how we feel at the moment, but a reflection of events as they are. So, for example, if a person feels fear because they see someone get off at the same low traffic stop on the train as they have, they will believe that the situation is inherently dangerous and the person wants to hurt them. This is not necessarily true. You have merely projected your emotions onto someone else. Another example is if you strongly dislike someone and reach the conclusion that "the two of you hate one another." Well, that is not necessarily true either. You have, again, projected your own feelings onto someone else.

Blaming

Blaming happens in people who tend to judge others (and themselves) harshly. As we have seen before, this is a characteristic of people who have an inferiority complex. If this applies to you, it would involve blaming others for something that does not go as you would like. You may even blame yourself. The question is not really who is at fault. The point is if anyone needs to be at fault at all. Things happen. Blaming yourself or others does not necessarily do you any good and it can be thought of as a cognitive distortion.

Shoulds

Shoulds are related to polarized thinking because these statements indicate a rigid, dogmatic way of viewing the world. Shoulds are statements or thoughts that involve the world should and imply how things ought to be (based on your own thinking). We can apply should statement to ourselves or to others. Should statements be distortions because they apply rules to the way that we behave when perhaps those rules do not apply? Should statements can cause us to feel anger at others and displeasure with ourselves.

Global Labeling

We all use labels, but it is easy for us to forget that words have power and can be used to harm others (or ourselves). Global labeling involves making a judgment based on one or two events. It is essentially an extreme type of overgeneralizing. So, someone who uses global labeling will use their experience with their last two boyfriends to say "all men are..." or "I am worthless." This is dysfunctional thinking because it can lead you to think negatively about yourself and others, which will lead you to behave based on these negative thoughts. You will never be able to live confidently if you make negative generalizations about events that happen to most people.

Magical Thinking

Magical thinking is both a type of cognitive distortion and a symptom of some conditions. In magical thinking, we think of things that have nothing to do with one another as being related. It is almost a type of superstitious thinking. For example, if someone rear-ends your car on the way home from work you think it is punishment for raising your voice at someone earlier that day. In reality, these events are completely unrelated. This type of thinking can be dysfunctional because it reflects a mind that is prone to feelings of guilt and shame or one that tends towards making judgments.

A Final Word about Cognitive Distortions

The term cognitive distortions mean precisely what the words in the term indicate – distorted thinking – but the point is not so much that the thinking is distorted, but that it is dysfunctional. We have mentioned the example of someone who has a bad encounter with another person – on the road, at work, or at a public place - and subsequently makes a generalization about all people. The truth is that generalizations are a way that we recognize patterns, which serve a role in guiding our behavior and protecting us. But these types of generalizations, even if sometimes true, become dysfunctional when they lower our self-esteem, isolate us, or prevent us from living happy lives.

The long and short of it is that cognitive distortions indicate a way of thinking that is not conducive to being happy and living confidently. You may have noticed that some of the happiest people may come across as being a little delusional. They may regard themselves as being more intelligent than they perhaps really are or better looking. We might say that they are overconfident. But guess what? These overconfident people apply for jobs and get them. They approach the men or women that they are interested in and get their offer for a date accepted.

Cognitive distortions are problematic because they trap us in a net of self-loathing, negative thinking, judgments of ourselves and others, isolation, disconnection, anxiety, and fear. As one psychoanalyst told a patient who was obsessed with the question of whether or not humans were good or evil or if the world was a good place: “What benefit does think about any of this do you?” Even if some of your negative thinking may be true some of the time, it does not do much benefit to you mulling it over, does it? Confident people do not spend their time mired in the negatives of their lives or of a particular situation and neither should you.

CHAPTER 6

Anxiety Triggers and Coping Skills

One of the things that makes anxiety so difficult to deal with is that it can be triggered by nearly anything. Indeed, anxiety, like depression, is associated with changes in brain chemistry as well as abnormal activation of certain areas of the brain (like the amygdala) so anxious people will feel just that because of triggers that would not normally make others anxious. In this chapter, we review some of the major triggers of anxiety as well as present some of the coping strategies to help readers remove this barrier to being self-confident.

Identifying Your Anxiety Triggers

Identifying your anxiety triggers will take some honesty on your part. Although many people with self-esteem issues, including anxious people, frequently have difficulty shining a mirror on themselves and seeing what they really look like it is necessary to do this in order to overcome this obstacle. How will you change those things about yourself that need to be changed if you do not first acknowledge them? If you want to be happy and you are not now then you will have to work for it.

Fortunately, overcoming anxiety and gaining confidence is not an insurmountable obstacle. Sometimes, the only thing that prevents people from being happy is themselves. Though you cannot control the things in your environment that trigger your anxiety, you can control how you manage them. Below is a list of some of the most common anxiety triggers. Afterward, each trigger will be discussed briefly.

- Stress from work
- Stress from school

- Economic insecurity
- Serious medical condition
- Relationship issues
- Substance use
- Medication side effect
- Grieving from a loss
- Social situations or crowds
- Being alone (isolation)

Stress from Work

Like it or not, most of us have to work and work environments can frequently be a source of stress in our lives. Leaving aside the reality that many people may have to work in occupations that they do not love, working also involves having to be in close proximity to other people and this can be a source of stress. Even people who do not have anxiety or another condition of mental health can feel stress from work, but when you already have an anxious temperament work the stressful nature of work can be nearly unbearable. The key to managing this particular trigger is not to avoid it altogether but to think about what precisely is it about the work environment that bothers you and how you might be able to manage it.

Stress from School

It is probably safe to say that as long as children (and adults) have been required to attend school there have been people stressed about school. School can be a particularly stressful environment, particularly for young people, because the school environment can sometimes bring out the worst people. Schools are characterized for being competitive and sometimes aggression or fear of it is at play. There is no shame in being triggered by the school, you just need to apply coping skills to manage your fears.

Economic Insecurity

It is a common concept in psychology that environmental stressors tend to exacerbate mental illness. Conversely, advantages tend to protect people from developing a mental illness or expressing one that they have a predisposition towards. Economic insecurity can be a huge trigger as it naturally brings along with it worries about the future. A poor economic situation will generate thoughts about how bills we paid, whether a move is necessary, will you have to seek help from others. It is not hard to understand how someone who is naturally anxious will be sent over the deep end because of these types of concerns.

Serious Medical Condition

Medical problems can also be very stressful. This is particularly the case in countries where medical care is very expensive and those suffering from illness have to deal with questions about how medical bills will be paid. Even leaving aside the financial side of things, medical woes bring with them fears about the future, loved ones, and the issue of death. A serious medical condition, therefore, represents not one trigger, but several all rolled into one.

Relationship Issues

Even people without anxiety or depression have difficulties dealing with the highs and lows of a relationship. It is not hard to understand why. We invest much of ourselves in our relationships with others. We lower our guard and open ourselves to be hurt. A failing relationship or issues of trust in a relationship can definitely trigger anxiety, depression, or both. Because of the nature of romantic relationships, putting anxiety coping skills to use here becomes a necessity for anxious people.

Substance Use

Unfortunately, many people who use (and abuse) substances do not recognize how these chemicals can trigger or worsen an underlying mental health condition or a disturbed mental state. If you are prone to excessive worry or panic attacks, certain substances can trigger your panic or anxiety symptoms, making life very uncomfortable for you. Although the natural solution is to discontinue using the substance, it is a reality that people can become addicted, particularly to substances like opiates, and getting off them is easier said than done. Substance abuse as a trigger for anxiety is really a Pandora's box of problems and people in this situation often need the help of a professional.

Medication Side Effect

Many medications can actually trigger panic attacks or other anxiety symptoms. Some medications that are particularly problematic include those given to treat thyroid problems or asthma. Men and women can also experience anxiety as a result of discontinuing an anxiety medication. Benzodiazepines, and particular, are a big culprit for severe anxiety symptoms when suddenly discontinued. If you take any medications and have started to feel anxious it may be worth examining whether the medication you take may be a cause.

Grieving from a Loss

Grief from death is associated with a whirlwind of feelings that can be anxiety-inducing. Those that grieve go through periods of denial and anger that eventually lead to acceptance, but on the way, much anxiety and depression can be experienced. Although this is a trigger that, like some of the others, you cannot avoid (as you cannot control the mortality of others), you can learn how to deal with it in a healthier way. If you need help from a professional, do not be too proud to seek the help you need.

Social Situations or Crowds

Anxiety over social situations really forces us to think about what is causing the anxiety in the first place. It is no coincidence that we discussed the inferiority complex before we delved into anxiety triggers as the unfortunate truth is that you may be anxious about being around others because you feel inferior. Or you may be anxious because you have experienced trauma and have trust issues. Whatever your particular scenario is, management of this trigger will require that you identify what it is exactly about social situations that trigger you. Though this may be a not particularly comfortable endeavor it will help you in the long run as you work on your confidence.

Being Alone (Isolation)

Being alone is tricky as it is a natural reaction for most people to retreat onto themselves when they feel threatened or unsafe. Just as an animal that has been wounded by a lion will find a safe place to rest and hide alone until they are better, so, too, do anxious people isolate themselves from others. But they do it because, at a certain level, they review the world and others in general as being threatening. It is interesting to think of the hikikomori again here as, though it may not be proven (or provable) that they have anxiety, there must certainly be an anxiety component to their hermitic state. If you are reading this, you probably do not want to be a hermit. Living like this will only worsen your anxiety because it gives you plenty of opportunities to worry about things and reinforces your threatening, negative perception of the world.

Finding the Right Coping Skills

Once you have a sense of what triggers your anxiety, you can start thinking about ways to cope with it. It does not do you any good to identify what you are anxious about and stop there. Your goal is to be confident and you will do that by first managing what is essentially keeping you from being confident. Anxiety not only lowers your self-esteem, but it can indicate that your self-esteem needs work, to begin with. There are many coping skills that you may be able to put to use in dealing with your anxiety, but here are some that we find particularly helpful.

- Starting a journal
- Schedule “worry time”
- Consider meditation, deep breathing, or other relaxation techniques
- Do things that make you happy

- Maintain supportive relationships and reach out when you are not feeling right
- Practice radical acceptance: accepting those things that may be unpleasant about yourself or others
- Eat healthy, less processed foods
- Remember how you have overcome hard times in the past
- Get plenty of sleep
- Avoid substances that can exacerbate anxiety and panic, like caffeine and alcohol
- Work together with a psychotherapist
- Be honest about your symptoms

Treatment for Anxiety

One of the goals of this book has been to help those who deal with anxiety as an impediment to their confidence to gain the skills that the need to overcome that anxiety. Having confidence allows men and women to live happy lives and the lack of it generally leads to dissatisfaction. Therefore, as much as a man or woman can be encouraged and guided to develop confidence, if anxiety is an issue then this must be dealt with, if not first, at least somewhere along the way. With that being said, many people are unable to handle their anxiety with coping skills and self-care alone. Such individuals benefit from anxiety treatment.

Treatment for anxiety can take many forms. Medication treatment is available to women and men that are anxious. Anxiolytics have been around for decades, and anxious persons also benefit from antidepressant medications. Indeed, because of the addictive nature of some anxiolytics, antidepressants are now commonly prescribed for anxiety as well. Another modality that has been shown to be highly beneficial to anxious persons is therapy. Both group therapy and individual therapy have proven beneficial to the anxious.

Individual therapy can be any of a variety of different types, including supportive psychotherapy, cognitive behavioral therapy, and dialectical behavioral therapy.

CHAPTER 7

The Importance of Self-Esteem and Confidence

People who have confidence have faith in themselves and believe that things will turn out favorably. It is sometimes said that confidence becomes a self-fulfilling prophecy as those that have it experience success because of their positive attitude rather than because of their ability while those who lack it create negative outcomes for themselves because they expect everything to turn out negatively. Lack of self-confidence becomes a problem when it guides people to behave in ways that actually sabotage their success and their happiness.

Self-esteem is a person's individual assessment of their own value or worth. It is entirely subjective, meaning that it is not a sort of resume that falls from the heavens that have an objective valuation of who we are. Self-esteem is what we think about ourselves. This means that it can be entirely true, entirely false, or somewhere in between. People who are narcissists have a grandiose, superior sense of self that is related to their underlying personality disorder while those who have low self-esteem generally see themselves as having less value than they really possess.

Why Self-Esteem and Confidence are Important

Self-esteem and confidence, therefore, are different though related concepts. We generally feel confidence, or lack it, based on our self-esteem. If we have a low opinion of ourselves then we will doubt our abilities and expect everything that we attempt to turn out poorly. If we have high self-esteem, we will be motivated to take risks because we know that things will turn out just as we want them to, and if they do not then we will try again.

Equipped with that explanation of self-esteem, it is not difficult to understand why this, along with confidence, is important. People who lack self-esteem will never try and achieve their dreams because they believe that they are incapable of success. They do not have confidence, trust, that they can achieve highly and that things will turn out well for them. Those, on the other hand, who do have confidence will enter every situation believing that things will turn out well.

Like it or not, as people we create a world of our own design. If we have a negative attitude, then the world around us and even our lives become negative. We experience failed relationships, failed jobs, and disappointment. We experience these not because the Fates decided that things must be this way, but because our negative thoughts and negative approach to life created a negative outcome. Someone who is confident approaches every situation with trust in themselves and the resilience to recover if things do not turn out exactly as planned. People like this do experience failures, but they experience more successes because their confidence permits them to take risks, to be natural and trusting around others, and to engage in life confident in the knowledge that matters will turn out well.

Is Overconfidence a Problem?

Overconfidence, the tendency to be more trusting in one's abilities or in the desired outcome than one has reason to expect, is found in some people. People who are overconfident can leap headfirst into situations where they should exercise caution, or take on roles that are completely outside of their abilities, which they have overestimated. They may propose marriage to the most beautiful woman at college because they are a little delusional about their own looks and charm.

Though it is not difficult to see how being overconfident can lead people into scrapes, actually, the most salient point here is that overconfidence can also lead such people to be more successful than those who are perhaps more capable, but less confident. In other words, nothing risked, nothing gained. No matter how great your abilities, looks, or other credentials are, you will not get anywhere in life unless you are willing to put yourself out there. You may be the most handsome guy (or girl) in school, but you are unlikely to go out on a date with the person you like unless you talk to them first.

Overconfident people can sometimes seem laughable because they expose themselves to the scrutiny and ridicule of others by acting outside of what may seem their natural place. In particular, people who lack self-esteem will be quick to judge overconfident people because they perceive a boldness in their behavior that they themselves lack and may even be a little envious (though they are unlikely to admit it). But as ridiculous as the overconfident folk may seem to some, for those who suffer from low self-esteem much can be learned by taking a page from their handbook.

Codependency and Unhealthy Relationships

It is helpful to talk about codependency in the context of confidence because people who are codependent often have low self-esteem, which is what lands them in the codependent relationship in the first place (and keeps them there). Also, existing in a codependent relationship will prevent you from gaining the self-esteem that you need to change your life. Let us start this short exploration by defining codependency. Codependent people enable the mental illness, addiction, or bad behavior of their partner. Such people also require the validation of others for their self-esteem. Codependency is a problem for a number of reasons, but partly because the partner of the codependent person traps them in an unhealthy relationship were emotional abuse and anguish become normal.

Because the codependent person needs their partner around in order to feel good about themselves, they often fall victim to partners who are abusive, neglectful, or just not worthy of them. Indeed, in the case of some codependent relationships, like the narcissistic relationship, the codependent person is deliberately targeted as a relationship partner because they are easy to abuse and are unlikely to leave. Again, the point here is that those dealing with issues of confidence need to examine if they are in a relationship that may be keeping their self-esteem low. The following are signs or traits of codependent people:

- Associating one's own self-worth with others
- Assuming the responsibility for meeting the needs of others
- Involving oneself with individuals that have personality disorders or addictions
- Being a prior victim of physical or sexual abuse
- The tendency towards anxiety and depression
- The tendency towards having negative thoughts and fears about separation

CHAPTER 8

Twelve Tips for Building Self-Esteem and Confidence

Many pages of this book have been spent on addressing those things that can prevent us from being confident and which cause us to have low self-esteem. Anxiety and depression are silent killers that weaken people often without their knowledge. An inferiority complex can cause us to have a negative view of ourselves and the world. And being in a codependent relationship can trap us in a cycle of low self-esteem and abuse, a pattern that only worsens if we do not recognize it. But now that we understand why we have low self-esteem and lack confidence we can begin to work towards remedying this situation. What follows are twelve tips that anyone can use to imbue their lives with a degree of confidence that they perhaps never thought possible.

Tip One: Engage in Activities That Make You Happy.

One thing that it is important to understand about confidence and happiness is that behaving as if we were happy - smiling and enjoying the company of others, etc. - will eventually lead us to feel happy all of the time. This is similar to what psychologists say about empathy. By practicing empathy, we eventually make empathy something natural and automatic in our lives. The same holds true for happiness. By engaging in activities that make us happy, practicing happiness, so to speak, we make happiness the norm in our lives, and with this happiness and peace will come confidence.

Tip Two: Recognize the Signs of Abuse and Codependency in Relationships and Take the Necessary Steps.

One of the most important things you can do to build self-esteem and confidence is to remove from your life those things that are sapping your self-esteem and confidence. Codependent relationships do just that. They trap you in a bond where you are not valued and where all of your actions serve only to enhance the value of your partner and enable their own dysfunction. By leaving, or in some cases, repairing, a codependent relationship you set yourself on the track towards feeling good about yourself.

Tip Three: Learn to Forgive Yourself Rather Than Feel Guilt and Shape.

There are certain behaviors that people who have a low sense of self-worth tend to engage in. One of these is that they are highly judgmental of themselves and of others. Although this can be a very hard habit to break, a good place to begin is to practice not being so hard on yourself. Confident people do not beat themselves up about their failures. They understand that failure is nothing more than an opportunity to shoot for something even better next time. If they allowed failures to hold them back, they would never get anywhere and the same holds true for you.

Tip Four: Learn That Your Own Needs Are Just as Important as the Needs of Others.

One thing that people who lack confidence (and are codependent) do is to place the needs and wellbeing of others above their own. Let us be clear here, no one is saying that you should be selfish or not care about others at all, but if you spent all your time caring about others you will not be able to meet your own needs. The analogy here is putting on the oxygen mask in an airplane that is experiencing a crash. You need to take care of your own oxygen before you can help anyone else.

Tip Five: Stop Comparing Yourself to Others.

Comparing oneself to others is a habit that most people do not realize is unhealthy. Indeed, comparing ourselves to those around us has become much easier (and depressing) in the day and age of cellphones, the internet, and social media. But when we compare ourselves to others, especially when we are anxious, all we do is find reasons to dislike ourselves. One thing that you can do is notice what others are doing, but ceasing comparing ourselves to them. If you want to compare yourself to anyone, compare yourself to, well, yourself.

Tip Six: Take a Long Hard Look in the Mirror and Learn to Love What You See.

This is one of the hardest lessons to learn. Many people who lack confidence run from their own reflection because they do not like what they may find staring back at them. This is understandable as no one is perfect and some people have life experiences that cause them to have a low opinion of themselves. But the cold, hard truth is that you will have to start loving yourself if you ever going to be confident. One thing that so-called overconfident people are good at is looking at the mirror and falling in love with the person reflected back at them even if what they see is not what others see.

Tip Seven: Practice Radical Acceptance.

Radical acceptance refers to accepting those things about yourself that are not perfect.

Therapists teach people that are depressed or anxious to practice radical acceptance as a tool for overcoming those things that may be causing them to feel the way they do. We all have things that we may not like about ourselves, but allowing them to drag us down will not get us anywhere. We have to learn to accept ourselves and others and move on.

Tip Eight: Stop Isolating Yourself. Go Out and Socialize.

Isolation is like a rabbit hole that never ends and becomes impossible to crawl out of. When we isolate ourselves, all we do is give an energy boost to the depression and anxiety that caused us to be isolated in the first place. Also, isolation reinforces our distorted belief that the world is a harmful, threatening place. You will never be successful or happy in life if you have this view. You will also never be successful in life if you never leave the house and do not know how to get on with other people. Like it or not, human beings are social creatures and if you want to be successful you will generally need others to help you get there. As much as you may want to isolate yourself at times, keep in mind that isolation will only make your lack of confidence worse, not better.

Tip Nine: Engage in Activities that Increase Your Release of Endorphins, Like Exercise.

This is a tip that anyone can use, which is why it is important to mention it here. Many of the other confidence tips require some thought and self-reflection, but exercise is something that you can just get out and do. Indeed, many people who are depressed self-manage their condition by engaging in activities like exercise. The positive endorphins that are released with exercise counteract the action of the neurotransmitters associated with depression and anxiety. When in doubt about what to do with your free time, go out and exercise.

Tip Ten: Meet the Things You Fear Head-On Rather than Continually Running from Them.

Related to isolation is the avoidant personality type. Anyone can fall victim to avoiding those things that bring unpleasantness into life. This may mean avoiding people or avoiding situations that cause us to feel uncomfortable. But if you are the type to fall victim to anxiety or depression, then most things can be unpleasant to you. Are you simply going to avoid everything? One thing that confident people do well is going out and meeting challenges head-on. Just as psychiatrists or psychotherapists will overcome phobias in clients by exposing them to their fears, so too will you have to learn to meet your fears and learn that there is less to be afraid of than you thought.

Tip Eleven: Practice Meditation and Other Grounding Techniques.

Meditation can be accomplished in several different ways. Some individuals engage in chanting, prayer, or deep breathing techniques. The reason why meditation is important - well, there are several, but one of the reasons - is because it grounds. It places us in the present rather than allowing us to focus on the past or in the future. Grounding calms us and allows us to let go of all of the things that can prevent us from behaving with confidence.

Tip Twelve: Learn to Take Risks.

Here is another tip that we can take from the handbook of the overconfident. Sure, risks can be scary because there is always a chance that you will fall flat on your face, but you certainly will not get anywhere if you remain planted where you are. The last thing you want is to live a life filled with regret that you never even tried the things that you wanted to do. Sure, you might fail, but the confident person learns not to feel failure but to learn from it.

CHAPTER 9: GETTING OUT OF A RUT

Every person experience being in a rut. Perhaps you used to be productive, energetic, and motivated to push forward, but suddenly something happens. You know longer feel the push to get from point A to point B like you used to. You do not have the energy that you used to have and the things that used to interest you no longer do so. Everything seems harder to do. If you are honest with yourself, you have to admit that you lack motivation. You are tired. These are the characteristic signs that you may be in a rut.

The reason why it is important to discuss getting out of a rut is that your issues with self-esteem may not be tied to more serious issues of anxiety, depression, or an inferiority complex. You might just be in a rut. When you are in a rut, you are no longer motivated like you used to be, but this does not necessarily mean that the particular conundrum that you find yourself in has to do with a mental health condition. In this chapter, we review the signs that indicate that you might be in a rut and discuss what you can do to get out of it.

What It Feels Like to Be in a Rut

Being in a rut is sort of like having writer's block except that you do not have to be a writer to experience it. When a writer has a block, they suddenly find that they are unable to write in the compelling way that they used to. The words on the page seemed forced and the writer will generally be dissatisfied with them because they know these words are not on par with what they have written before and what they are capable of.

In Camus's *The Plague*, the author describes a curious character who longs to finish his novel, but cannot get past the first page. He has written the first sentence of his revolutionary novel over and over for several years but cannot resist the urge to rewrite it. When someone has a block or is in a rut, it is like their ability of speech has suddenly been taken out of their mouths. And as in many novels where the mute person really has a psychological reason for why they are mute rather than a physical one, the same can generally be said for ruts.

People who are in a rut generally have something in their brain that is mentally keeping them from finishing the task. Perhaps they are going through a midlife crisis. Perhaps they are distracted by other events going on in their life. Perhaps they are afraid of the consequences that will come from finally completing the task. Sometimes the issue is that they have lost their confidence, an issue that is frequently behind the writer's block that even the best authors experience.

Ruts can impact your life greatly because they can creep out of the realm where they began and take over your life. So, perhaps you rut began with you pushing back the ETA on your big project at work. But now you have stopped going to the gym, are getting up later and later, and have decided to drop the night classes you were taking to get your master's degree. You are in a rut.

Many, if not most, people who are in a rut have an underlying confidence issue. Perhaps they no longer feel up to the tasks that they normally feel up to, but even if someone does not feel comfortable admitting that their issue is one of confidence it is helpful for such people to at least admit that they are at a valley in their lives rather than a peak and need to think about what to do. With the goal of helping such people recognize that they are in a run, the following is a brief list of some signs that indicate that this may apply to you.

- You are unproductive
- You show a lack of energy
- You are inconsistent in your performance
- You are not getting your work in on time
- You are eating more unhealthy foods
- You are less physically active
- This pattern can last for weeks and weeks

Getting Out of a Rut Fast

Getting out of a rut does not necessarily require that you try to unearth why you are in a rut in the first place. It can help, but if you are like most people you do not have the time and your primary focus is just to get out of the rut (not spend time thinking about how it came about). In fact, because ruts are a common part of life this may be an instance where you can leave the psychoanalysis to someone else. If your steps to get out of a rut, which we will review below, do not help then you can put more work into thinking about the cause.

So how do you get out of a rut? One thing to keep in mind in attempting to get out of a rut is that this process is more physical than cerebral. Building confidence can be a cerebral process, but for many people, the best course of action is just that: action. Below is a list of steps that can be taken to get even the most deeply in a rut person out of that predicament (with explanations to follow).

- Give yourself rewards for small steps
- Go out and do something
- Work your way towards more action

- Learn to manage your expectations

Some people do not like the practice of giving themselves rewards for the baby steps they have accomplished, but let's face it. Positive reinforcement is a thing because it works. We use it on our pets. We use it for our children. Use it on yourself. Rather than laying around watching television and eating potato chips because you are not motivated to do anything, make a list of things that you have to do and then reward yourself for each thing that you accomplish.

This first step in getting out of a rut naturally gives way to the next one. Go out and do something. Going out and engaging in activities works because it operates on the action/motivation cycle. Instead of having the motivation to do an action, you can actually use the performance of an action to create motivation for future action. Yes, it may sound a little unusual to those who have not tried it before, but it is a way of tricking the brain and it works.

Taking action does not end with the first action that you take. That first step allows you to work your way towards more action. So, when you decide to stop being a slob and to go out and do one thing you need to do, you will find that it is easier to go on and do more things. If we are being psychoanalytical, we can say that completing that first action is increasing your self-esteem and building your confidence, which is the overall goal, but if it helps you to think of this as just getting out of a rut then go for it.

Learning to manage your expectations is last on the list of steps, but it is far from the least important. Many people are in a rut because, for whatever reason, they have become subconsciously overwhelmed by the expectations of themselves and others. They may believe themselves unable to complete the accruing list of tasks and obligations ahead of them so they lose interest altogether. Practicing having realistic expectations and not allowing yourself to overthink things is, for many people, the key to getting out of a rut and staying out of it.

CHAPTER 10
Communication Skills to Build Confidence

Human beings are not meant to live in isolation. Even our nearest relatives, the primates of jungles around the world, exist in social groups that function with complex layers of relationships. The same is true of human beings only we use communication to establish these relationships and to operate within the overarching structure of the society. What this means for you is that good communication skills are an essential tool to have if you hope to achieve success. The success that comes with knowing how to communicate effectively will inspire confidence, creating a positive loop of decisive action (in the form of communication) and confidence.

The relationship between confidence and communication is interesting because confidence is needed for good communication, but successful communication inspires confidence. An effective step that those wanting to quickly experience the benefits of confidence can try is to be more outgoing with their communication. Strike up conversations with people, call people you have not spoken to in a while. These are all ways that you can create a feedback loop of communication and confidence that will show results right away.

With that said, the primary focus of this chapter is actually to analyze the different styles of communication, in particular, styles that are often ineffective and can be dysfunctional. Aggressive communication and passive communication are two styles of communicating that are much more problematic than they might at first appear to the casual observer. On the other hand, assertive communication is what most people should shoot for. This is a style in which we are able to express our opinions and stand up for ourselves without starting conflict.

Aggressive Communication

It is easy to confuse being assertive with being aggressive as both involve standing up for oneself. The difference between being assertive and being aggressive is that aggressive behavior can often become physical and can damage relationships, while assertive communication is primarily intended to get your point across in situations where it may be difficult to do so.

Indeed, aggressive, and assertive communication is quite different. It actually takes confidence to be assertive because when you are assertive you are placing your trust in yourself and others as well as having confidence that you will not end up on the short end of the stick. It is important to learn how to communicate assertively rather than aggressively as the altercations and damaged relationships that come from aggression actually create negative outcomes that lower your self-esteem and harm your confidence. What are some of the primary differences between aggressive and assertive communication? Below is a list of the major bullet points.

- Aggressive communication can lead to physical confrontations while assertive communication generally does not.
- Assertive communication leaves the door open for compromise while aggressive communication does not.
- Aggressive communication can involve pushing others around or bullying them while assertiveness is merely intended to communicate information respectfully.

- In aggressive communication, only the wants or needs of the aggressive party matter while in assertive communication the needs of both are valued.
- Aggressive communication frequently damages relationships, burning bridges that it can be difficult to repair.

Passive Communication

Passive communication is on the opposite end of the spectrum from aggressive communication although it is just as big of a problem. When we are passive, we allow others to force their needs and opinions on ourselves while our own needs go unmet. Passive people do not speak up for themselves. When they do speak, they may use a soft voice or have body language that indicates submission. This is not helpful either in communication or in being confident as being passive and submissive merely gives others the opportunity to force their opinions on you. Another sign of being passive is using language that defers to others such as "only if it is okay" or "if you do not mind." Another troublemaker is "It does not really matter to me."

Passive communication can be damaging to your self-esteem because it creates a pattern where the passive individual is always the lesser partner in interactions. Being passive also creates problems in relationships. Passiveness also can lead to anger because of feelings that one is being ignored, bullied, or otherwise taken advantage of. By being assertive, you allow your thoughts to be known to others and embark on the destination of greater self-esteem.

Tips for Being Assertive

Being assertive is one of the quickest ways to develop confidence. When you are assertive, you are more likely to get what you want and that creates trust in yourself and in life that things will work out in positive ways, which is really what confidence is. Below is a list of tips to help you be more assertive.

- Do not shout or whisper, but speak in a normal tone of voice.
- Communicate what you want honestly and sincerely.
- Looking at the floor or otherwise avoiding eye contact is a no-no. Look other straight in the eye with a relaxed face.
- Do not communicate with judgments as these can be construed as being aggressive. Stick solely to the facts.
- Try to make sure that your body language matches the words that you are saying. If you are being sincere and respectful but your body language indicates aggression or distance then

this will impact how what you say is perceived.

- Practice being assertive until it becomes second nature to you.

CHAPTER 11

Tips for Dealing with Anxiety

Rome was not built in a day and confidence also will not be gained in such a short span of time. There are many tools that you can use to gain confidence, and these begin with getting better at dealing with anxiety. These tips are not solely for those who label themselves as being anxious or have been diagnosed as such. You may be surprised to find that even though you never thought anxiety was an issue for you these tips speak to you.

Tip One: Understand That the Feeling Is Not the Problem, It Is What You Do with It.

Psychotherapists frequently tell their patients that it isn't the feelings they have that are a problem. It's what they do with them. This comes up because anxious and depressed people often feel guilt and shame around their feelings. They may ruminate for hours or even days about commonplace events. The step to changing this dynamic is not to run away from the feelings but to claim them. There is nothing wrong with your anxiety or any other feeling you have. Use those feelings as motivation.

Tip Two: Recognize Dysfunctional Thoughts and Redirect.

The trick of mindfulness involves being aware of your thoughts. This self-awareness allows you to constantly be in touch with yourself so that you track negative thoughts before they spiral out of control. Something as simple as someone not greeting you can quickly morph into feelings of anger and shame. This is basically the cognitive distortions of personalizing and magnifying. Try to catch yourself doing this and redirect your thoughts somewhere else.

Tip Three: Get Out More.

It is impossible to overstate how bad isolation is for anxiety and low self-esteem. Although isolation may seem like the natural thing to do when you are not feeling well, people who are anxious, in a rut, or lacking in self-esteem can frequently find themselves feeling low and so they spend most of their time isolated. All this isolation does is magnify whatever thoughts or feelings are keeping you isolated. Break the isolation by going out.

Tip Four: Stop Seeing Things in Black and White.

Black and white thinking is oh so common. Indeed, even some religions promote the idea that life exists in neat, dichotomous divisions of black and white. But what this black and white thinking does is encourage you to judge yourself and others unfairly. No one is perfect. Indeed, many of the things you and others do are probably not that bad. When you judge others and yourself, you can act in anger and ill will. These behaviors damage relationships, create negative outcomes, hurt other people, and only give you more reasons to be anxious.

Tip Five: Recognize that No One is Perfect.

No one is perfect and that includes you. Once you realize that you are not the only one who is not perfect you will stop being so hard on yourself. Indeed, learning to love yourself frequently involves developing a more accurate perception of others. Recognizing that no one is perfect actually helps your confidence because it leads you to realize that you are not much different from others.

Tip Six: Engage in Activities that Ground you Like Meditation.

Meditation grounds you. Grounding in this context means bringing your mind to the present. People with anxiety and depression tend to focus on the traumatic events of the past and the worries about the future. Grounding activities allow you to focus your mind solely on what is happening right now. Notice the chirp of the birds or the fall colors. Meditation will help you.

Tip Seven: Consider Enlisting the Help of Others If You Are Having Difficulty Changing Your Thoughts.

Going over your thoughts and worries with other people is more helpful than many realize. It is easy to go down a rabbit hole of stress and angst, not really understanding that your fears and worries are all in your head. By bouncing your thoughts off of others, you get a more realistic sense of what is going on in your world.

Tip Eight: Reality Test to Determine if Your Anxiety is Realistic.

Reality testing is a way of comparing your thoughts to what is actually going on. This is an important step because confident, successful people do not have the time to waste worrying about things that are not actually happening. Are you worried that you might lose your job? What evidence do you have that this is really a possibility? If you are basing it solely on the fact that your boss was grumpy this morning then your worries may be all in your head.

Tip Nine: Engage in Radical Acceptance.

Radical acceptance means accepting those things that you cannot change about yourself and about others. This not only helps us to gain confidence, but it can also improve our relationships with others. Improved relationships with others actually help to boost our confidence by giving us the subconscious feeling that we have the support of others.

Tip Ten: Consider Getting Professional Help if All Else Fails.

If all else fails, consider seeking the help of someone with advanced training. Unfortunately, anxiety is an epidemic for good reason. Many people are not able to pull themselves out of the cycle of worry and fear. Sometimes advanced treatment like medication, therapy, or other modalities is needed and a doctor can point you in the right direction for help.

CHAPTER 12

5 Ways Self-Confidence Will Change Your Life

Self-confidence opens doors that were once tightly shut and locked. If we do not have self-confidence, we are unable to truly love others because we never give freely of ourselves. We keep a part of ourselves shut out of interactions as we fear what others would think if they saw the true us. Gaining confidence truly is life-changing. Below is a list of five ways that confidence can change your life.

- Better relationships with friends and family
- More drive to succeed at work
- Humility
- Failures become easier to stomach
- Freedom

Way #1: Better Relationships with Friends and Family.

Behaving with confidence will lead to improvements in all of your relationships, including your romantic ones. Other people can tell when you are behaving with sincerity and self-love, and they respond to it. When you have a low opinion of yourself or feel insecure, this is detected by others and it engenders the same feelings in them. If you do not believe in yourself then why should anyone else believe in you? Once you have developed confidence, others will gravitate towards you and your relationships will improve.

Way #2: More Drive to Succeed at Work.

Many people find themselves in a rut and never figure out just what it was that put them there. Although someone in a rut does not necessarily have to admit that their problem is one of confidence, anecdotal evidence suggests that having confidence allows people to make changes in life that move them forward. In short, confidence gives people the motivation that they lack when they are in a rut. This particular claim is not anecdotal: people who are more confident tend to have more success at work.

Way #3: Humility.

We may not think of humility and confidence as going hand in hand, but they do, in fact, go hand in hand. It is hard to be humble when you do not like yourself very much. Being humble requires that you allow yourself to be taken down a peg and it is hard if not impossible to do that if you already perceive yourself as being at the bottom rung of the ladder. Confidence and, importantly, self-esteem allow us to be humble and benefit from all of the joy that comes from giving in this way.

Way #4: Failures Become Easier to Stomach.

Everyone has failures. Like it or not, this is a part of life. But what distinguishes successful people from those who are less successful is how failures are managed. People who lack confidence have a hard time picking themselves back up and getting going again because they have no faith, or trust, that things will work in their favor. Conversely, confident people know that it is only a matter of time before things turn around.

Way #5: Freedom.

Every man and woman want to be free. In the context of confidence, freedom means the ability to do all of the things you have ever wanted to do without being weighed down by unnecessary fear, worries, or self-doubt. Gaining confidence will set you free from everything that is holding you back in life. All it takes is a little bit of confidence and you will be free to choose your own path. You will be fearless should that path meander in a different direction. Of all the things that confidence can bring, perhaps nothing is as valuable as that.

FREQUENTLY ASKED QUESTIONS

1. **What is confidence and why is it important to have confidence?**

   Confidence means to have trust in oneself and to believe that things will work out as expected. Confidence comes from a Latin word, which means to trust or to have faith in. Confidence is necessary to live a happy and fulfilled life. People who lack confidence never pursue their dreams because they are afraid of failure. Having confidence has also been linked to success in jobs and relationships.

2. **What role does anxiety have in confidence?**

Anxiety prevents people from behaving with confidence. People who are anxious view the world in a fearful, negative way, which disallows them from having trust in themselves, others, and the world. A common aspect of anxiety is negative thoughts that cause anxious people to interpret everyday events in threatening, negative ways. Overcoming anxiety, therefore, becomes essential in gaining confidence for many people.

3. **What is generalized anxiety disorder and how is it diagnosed?** There are several conditions referred to as anxiety disorders of which generalized anxiety disorder, or GAD, is only one. GAD is very common, impacting about 3% of individuals in the United States in any given year. Phobias are also regarded as anxiety disorders and some have argued that

these may be even more common than GAD. The criteria used in the DSM-5 to make a diagnosis of GAD include the following:

- Excessive anxiety or worry that lasts more than six months. This worry is present the majority of the time across many activities.
- Inability to manage symptoms of anxiety
- The presence of three or more of the following:
- Difficulty sleeping
- Irritable mood
- Difficulty concentrating
- Easily fatigued
- Tension in the muscles
- Restlessness
- Anxiety symptoms are dysfunctional

- Anxiety symptoms are not related to taking medication, substance, or another medical problem
- Anxiety symptoms are not better accounted for by another diagnosis, like post-traumatic stress disorder or panic disorder

4. **What are cognitive distortions? Why is it important to overcome cognitive distortions in order to gain confidence?**

Cognitive distortions are a way of thinking negatively and they are caused by interpreting events in exaggerated or unrealistic ways. Cognitive distortions serve the role of reinforcing the negative perceptions and life outcomes associated with anxiety. People who are unable to recognize and change cognitive distortions are unlikely to be able to gain the confidence that will result in life change. Through cognitive distortions, anxious people create a world that is filled with anger and hostility. They create this world interpreting events such that they always fit their perceptions. People who think this way do not realize that they have constructed around themselves a world that I will be impossible for them to live in.

5. **How does someone end up in a rut and how do they get out of one?**

Someone who is in a rut usually loses the motivation to complete a task, a lack of drive that eventually seeps into the rest of their life. Ruts can last for weeks or even months. People who are in a rut often have something mentally blocking them from finishing the task.

They may be distracted by events in their life or going through a midlife crisis.

Many people who are in a rut have an underlying confidence issue. They may no longer feel up to the tasks that they would typically have no problem with. The good thing about addressing ruts is that this action does not require that you become a psychoanalyst and figure out why you are in the rut in the first place. Actions come in handy here to literally pull you out of a rut. Below is a list of steps that can help.

- Give yourself rewards for small steps
- Go out and do something
- Work your way towards more action
- Learn to manage your expectations

6. What are the main types of cognitive distortions?

Cognitive distortions are dysfunctional ways of interpreting otherwise ordinary events. The main types of cognitive distortions include:

- Filtering
- Black and white thinking
- Magnifying
- Minimizing
- Personalizing
- Overgeneralization
- Catastrophizing
- Jumping to conclusions
- Fallacy of control (external locus of control vs internal control)
- Fallacy of fairness
- Emotional reasoning (I feel this way so it must be true)
- Blaming

- Shoulds
- Global labeling
- Magical thinking

7. What is an inferiority complex and what does it have to do with confidence?

An inferiority complex is an exaggerated sense that one is less than others. It is often combined with a pessimistic attitude about life. Prominent psychoanalysts have posited that humans are motivated to develop and achieve by an inferiority complex. In particular, a psychoanalyst named Alfred Adler, a student of Sigmund Freud argued that inferiority complexes are present in all infants and are a spur for normal development.

The inferiority complex is important to understand as it may be lurking in the background on issues of low confidence and self-esteem. Though many people may not admit that they have an inferiority complex, such a state can naturally persist from childhood into adulthood in those who have a disability or handicap, those who have been abused or neglected, or those who have faced social and economic hardship. Although many people naturally use that inferiority complex to achieve highly and change their circumstances some are not able to do so. Indeed, such people may not recognize that they feel this way, creating a monkey on the back, so to speak, that always impacts their ability to reach their goals.

8. **Are there signs that can clue someone in that they have an inferiority complex?**

People who feel inferior look just like everyone else. Indeed, you may be surprised that people you thought were “perfect” or “have it easy” might actually be dealing with this type of issue. In fact, some people work hard to overcome their inferiority complex, which can lead them to present an image of perfection to the outside world. There are many signs that someone may be dealing with an inferiority complex and below are some of the more common ones.

- You are highly judgmental of others (criticizing others and finding fault with them)
- You have intense feelings of guilt, shame, and envy
- You have a false, inflated sense of superiority (trying hard to hide one’s own inferiority)

- You are prone to passive behaviors and overall procrastination
- You feeling a strong need to please others and fit into the crowd
- You perceive others as a threat to yourself
- You are highly sensitive to criticism
- You withdraw from society or engage in attention-seeking behaviors
- You comparing yourself to others to your disadvantage

9. How can an inferiority complex be overcome?

The good thing is, an inferiority complex does not have to last a lifetime. Inferiority complexes can be overcome. In fact, if you believe that every person is born with an inferiority complex than the fact of the matter is most people are able to overcome this. The following is a list of tips that can help you overcome an inferiority complex if you believe that you have one (and many of us do).

- Do not compare yourself to others; instead, compare yourself to yourself
- Try to identify the cause of your feelings of inferiority so you can debunk them
- Think about who you feel inferior to and in which social situations
- Redirect your negative, dysfunctional thoughts into more helpful ones
- Do not be a perfectionist, it will not get you anywhere

- Learn to accept yourself for you who are through self-awareness, meditation, and other activities
- Try to have people around you who are supportive and warm
- Learn to love yourself by reminding yourself what is good about you
- Do not use the values of other people as a measuring stick for your own self-worth

10. What are some coping strategies that can help me manage my anxiety?

There are many coping skills available to help you overcome your anxiety and become confident. It may be helpful for you to think about what triggers your anxiety and come up with some specific strategies just for you. Here are some other strategies that may be of use.

- Starting a journal and writing in it daily
- Schedule “worry time”
- Consider meditation, deep breathing, or other relaxation techniques
- Do things that make you happy
- Maintain supportive relationships and reach out when you are not feeling right
- Practice radical acceptance: accepting those things that may be unpleasant about yourself or others
- Eat healthy, less processed foods
- Remember how you have overcome hard times in the past
- Get plenty of sleep

- Avoid substances that can exacerbate anxiety and panic, like caffeine and alcohol
- Work together with a psychotherapist
- Be honest about your symptoms

CONCLUSION

Confidence is a quality that every man and woman need to infuse their life with happiness. Confidence allows you to enter encounters equipped with the knowledge that you are capable to overcome any situation and that matters will unfold in a favorable way. Confidence literally means to trust: to trust yourself, that you have the abilities needed to pull through, and to trust life, that it will play out fairly and positively.

Living in a day and age where there is no privacy: where everyone is interconnected and one simple slip up or misunderstanding can wind up on the permanent record that is the internet, in this day and age it is easy to have worries and fears. Indeed, nearly half a million people in Japan have embarked on a life of nearly total social isolation: the so-called hikikomori. These individuals have turned away from work obligations, school, and personal relationships outside of the family. It is safe to say that they have found the world too unfriendly for them to be capable of navigating it safely.

In fact, studies suggest that anxiety is not only a peculiar characteristic of Western, developed nations but that it is on the rise. Although technology that improves our capacity to communicate with each other was designed to make our leaves easier, for millions of people it has made their lives harder. A life where we are all on display and our actions are instantly compared to those of others, that life is a little more difficult, which makes confidence a little harder to come by.

But confidence can change your life if you let it. Men and women who are confident are more successful at their jobs, have a better romantic and other relationships, are better at communicating and have a higher quality of life. Confident people are able to push the negative, distracting thoughts that occasionally creep up to the side, focusing solely on what is positive. We gain confidence by practicing being confident: taking ourselves out of isolation, interacting with others, learning not to judge ourselves or others, and radically accepting the world for what it is. Equipped with this attitude, you will rapidly gain confidence and watch as the puzzle pieces of happiness fall into place.

DESCRIPTION

Confidence can be elusive for many, but it is vital to living a happy, healthy life. As the modern world becomes more interconnected with digital technology, the ability to enter social situations with self-esteem and confidence becomes essential not just for happiness, but for survival. A person who does not acknowledge the importance of having confidence in social situations puts themselves at risk for living in isolation. In *Confidence Changed My Life*, readers will learn why confidence is so important for contentment and to achieve success.

One of the most important tools for gaining confidence is recognizing that confidence problems may stem from anxiety. Anxiety is one of the most frequent reasons patients visit their primary care physician, although many people do not realize that what they are suffering from is anxiety. Excessive worries and fears have become an issue impacting millions in the developed world. It is estimated that approximately four percent of adults will deal with significant anxiety at some point in their life, and the number of affected individuals is even higher in some countries. In *Confidence Changed My Life*, readers will learn to recognize the signs and symptoms of anxiety in order to determine if worries play a role in their life.

Confidence refers to the ability to trust in one's own abilities and that things will turn out as expected. Self-esteem is one's intrinsic sense of self-worth, that one has value. Anxious people frequently lack trust in their abilities, expect events to turn out poorly, and have a low sense of self-worth relative to others. What this means is that, for such people, building confidence begins with eradicating anxiety. This can be a sticking point for some as they may be reluctant to label themselves as being anxious, but accomplishing this step is the beginning of turning your life around. In *Confidence Changed My Life*, readers will learn how combating anxiety really can be life-changing.

Once the causes of low self-esteem and a lack of confidence have been identified, that is when the real work begins: building confidence. We sometimes poke fun at overconfident people because they seem out of touch with reality and expose themselves to ridicule, but most people would benefit from taking a page from the handbook of the overconfident. Readers of *Confidence Changed My Life* will learn how qualities, like having a positive attitude, seeing the upside of things, seeing failures as opportunities for further success, and taking risks, are traits of the overconfident that are tied to success and happiness.

The truth is that it can be hard to be confident and in today's world where we are constantly exposed to what others are doing this seems to be getting even harder. But changing your life with confidence is closer than it seems. In *Confidence Changed My Life*, the following topics designed to help readers develop the skills they need to change their lives will be covered:

- The ways anxiety impacts your life
- The fear pathway in the brain
- Overcoming negative thinking
- Why self-esteem and confidence are important
- Codependency and unhealthy relationships
- Tips for being assertive
- Getting out of a rut
- Steps to reduce anxiety and build self-confidence

Printed in Great Britain
by Amazon